S0-ACM-155

JOHN COLTRANE

a Sound Supreme

JOHN SELFRIDGE

Introduction by

BRANFORD MARSALIS

Franklin Watts
A Division of Scholastic Inc.
New York • Toronto • London • Auckland • Sydney
Mexico City • New Delhi • Hong Kong
Danbury, Connecticut

To Dad

. . . a jazz lover, who first played the music for me
and whose favorites I'll always hear in my head.
—J.W.S.

Cover illustration by Greg Christie, interpreted from a photograph by ©Chuck Stewart.
Cover design by Ox and Company Interior design by Molly Heron

Photographs©: AP/Wide World Photos: 49; Chuck Stewart: 36, 60; Corbis-Bettmann: 32 (Frank Driggs);
Courtesy of Atlantic Records: 55 (Lee Friedlander); Courtesy of Sony Music Entertainment Inc.: 58
(Jay/Maisel Manufactured by Columbia Records); Courtesy of the High Point Museum, High Point, NC:
19; Courtesy of the Universal Music Group: 77 (MCA/Impulse); Duncan Schiedt: 64; Frank Driggs
Collection: 71 (Joe Alper); 52; Mosaic Images: 84 (Francis Wolff); Raymond Ross Photography: 82;
Retna Ltd./Camera Press Ltd.: 40 (David Redfern), 44 (Redferns/Bob Willoughby); Yasuhiro Fujioka
Collection: 12 (Courtesy of Michelle Coltrane), 80 (Kazuo Arai), 28 (Bill Goldstein), 8 (Roger Kasparian),
76 (Hozumi Nakadaira), 17, 41, 83.

Library of Congress Cataloging-in-publication Data
Selfridge, John W.
    John Coltrane : a sound supreme / John Selfridge ; introduction by Brandford Marsalis.
        p. cm.
    Discography: p. 90
    Includes bibliographical references and index.
    Summary: Traces the life of the innovative jazz saxophonist and the evolution of his music.
        ISBN 0-531-11542-9 (lib. bdg.)   0-531-16408-X (pbk.)
        1. Coltrane, John, 1926-1967 Juvenile literature. 2. Jazz musicians--United States Biography
Juvenile literature. [1. Coltrane, John, 1926-1967. 2. Musicians. 3. Jazz. 4. Afro-Americans Biography.] I.
Title.
    ML3930.C535S45 1999
    788.7'154'092--dc21
    [B]   99-22679
                                                                              CIP

©1999 Franklin Watts, a Division of Scholastic Inc.
All rights reserved. Published simultaneously in Canada.
Printed in Mexico
    5 6 7 8 9 10 R 08 07 06

CONTENTS

INTRODUCTION

Without a doubt, John Coltrane stands as one of the most profoundly influential musicians of the twentieth century.

The influence of John Coltrane's music extends well beyond the world of jazz. The composer/conductor Leonard Bernstein, for example, could often be seen at Coltrane performances during the 1960s. In The Doors' 1967 recording of "Light My Fire," the vamp section is clearly a paean to John Coltrane's 1960s quartet. Also, the Jimi Hendrix Experience drummer Mitch Mitchell's use of triplet-based fills is a tribute to the dynamic playing style of Coltrane quartet drummer Elvin Jones. While I was recording with Crosby, Stills, and Nash in 1990, David Crosby told me about the first time he heard John Coltrane in concert and the lasting effect that experience had on him. Even James Brown, the "Godfather of Soul," can be heard, during a recorded performance of his song "Super Bad," to cry out to his saxophone player, "Blow me some Trane!"

John Coltrane's music was always a work in progress, as is evident throughout Coltrane's body of recorded work. Coltrane's playing on the Miles Davis Prestige recordings reflects a completely different approach than his mid-1960s performances for Atlantic Records, and these performances are strikingly different than those he did for the Impulse! label toward the end of his life.

Coltrane's music can be technically complex, and so a true appreciation of it is something that must be acquired over time. I first heard John Coltrane's music when I was a teenager and my father played me the album entitled *John Coltrane*. I was so intimidated by the sound that almost five years went by before I tried to listen to Coltrane again!

In retrospect, I realize that I failed to appreciate Coltrane's music at the tender age of fifteen because I hadn't yet acquired the sensibility prerequisite to an appreciation of modern art. American popular culture—which tends to be defined and driven by each generation of teenagers and young adults—is today, perhaps more than ever, characterized by excess and immediacy. Aided by a wide range of media available in our information-saturated culture, we are a culture that has come to demand instant gratification in all aspects of life, and the offerings of our culture are mostly aimed at meeting that demand. However, there is no shuttle train to a true appreciation of great art. The works of modern artists like Pablo Picasso, Richard Strauss, Igor Stravinsky, Charlie Parker, Ernest Hemingway, Langston Hughes, or John Coltrane can't be appreciated without some combination of experience, maturity, patience, concentration . . . and, yes, study—not only of the works themselves, but also of the work that came before. To gain a true appreciation, you have to start at the very beginning and slowly work your way up.

This is not to say that the music of John Coltrane hasn't had and won't have an immediate effect on some listeners. On the contrary, even on first hearing, his music can be very seductive, especially for those with some experience listening to improvisational music. Perhaps what strikes the listener immediately about Coltrane's music is the uniquely emotional quality of his sound. Throughout his life, Coltrane was so engaged in the creative process that his growth as a musician closely paralleled his own personal and spiritual development. For this reason, there is an emotional depth to Coltrane's music, an almost unearthly quality to his tone, that can leave the listener stunned, if not thoroughly seduced and moved in extraordinary ways.

I've no opinion as to where jazz is in the hierarchy of musical forms—or even if there is such a hierarchy—but jazz is definitely the most difficult music I've attempted to play. This difficulty lies partly in the fact that, at its best, jazz is the musical lineage between art and popular expression. Having devoted myself to a life in music, and struggled with playing jazz from a very young age, I am, of course, humbled by the achievements of jazz masters such as John Coltrane, but I'm also inspired by them. And this inspiration carries over not only into my own music but into all aspects of my life.

The musician and non-musician alike will be inspired by the life and music of John Coltrane. For him, music and life were one and the same. With every note he played, Coltrane was deeply involved in the process of making music that was true to his being. From this we can all learn something of great value for our own lives.

—Branford Marsalis

CHAPTER ONE
LIVE AT THE FIVE SPOT

*T*he Bowery section of New York City is and, it seems, always has been, a shadowy, seedy, and even scary part of town. But that never stopped the lines from forming early at the front door of the Five Spot when pianist Thelonious Monk was on the bill.

Monk was a recluse. Sure, you could call him up at any time, day or night; he was usually awake, and his number was in the New York City phone book. But most of the time that would not have been a good idea; telephone etiquette was not Monk's thing. His thing was knockin' 'em dead at the Five Spot, and that is where you would have to go to catch him.

Monk's music—jagged, complex, spontaneous, abrupt, raw, and yet always swinging—was decades ahead of its time. One defining characteristic of his music was Monk's use of wide intervals between notes and chords in his compositions; another was the frequent use of irregular, syncopated rhythms, where the upbeats are accented. Musicians loved to play with Monk because they would learn so much; he was a sort of jazz guru. But not many players could meet the demands of performing Monk's music. The technical difficulty of his compositions exhausted his fellow band members physically, and his way of going with his own brilliant musical whims kept them on edge through every set. After a show they needed hours to wind down. The state of musical tension Monk created onstage always resulted in a night of exhilarating music, performed with a kind of calculated abandon, a reckless precision.

Before Monk first took the stage at the Five Spot, it was just like any other small bar in New York and perhaps a little darker and dingier than most. But Monk's debut put the Five Spot on New York City's musical map, establishing the club as one of the great jazz venues of the 1950s and 1960s. In June 1957, as Monk prepared to take the stage at the Five Spot for what seemed the hundredth time, the line of jazz fans snaked around the block hours before show time.

Saxophonist John Coltrane had not yet acquired the international following he would eventually enjoy. Although he was well known on the American jazz scene as a sideman, particularly as a result of his work with trumpeter/composer Miles Davis, Coltrane had received mixed reactions from the jazz critics thus far in his career. But his fellow musicians knew better than the critics. Most of them, including Monk, considered Coltrane one of the most innovative young saxophonists on the jazz scene.

Monk and Coltrane had recently run into each other while the sax player was working with Miles Davis, a sometimes brash and always extremely demanding bandleader. Miles's group was playing at the Bohemia, another New York jazz club, and Monk dropped by to say hello. Backstage, Miles and John got into an argument, which resulted in Coltrane getting a slap in the face and a punch in the stomach from the hot-tempered bandleader. Coltrane dismissed the matter as a simple misunderstanding, but Monk was outraged. He approached the tenor player and said, "As much saxophone as you play, you don't have to take that. Why don't you come to work for me?" With the addition of Wilbur Ware on bass and Shadow Wilson on drums, one incarnation of the Thelonious Monk Quartet was born.

With Coltrane and Monk working in tandem, the quartet consistently pushed their creative energy to great heights, and the crowds returned night after night, week after week. The sets consisted almost entirely of Monk compositions, such as "Blue Monk," "Criss Cross," and "Epistrophy," but the band would typically cover a few standards in each set as well. Often the patrons would get up and dance to the music. Sometimes, after his solo, Monk would lay out and "stroll," joining the dancing crowd and leaving Coltrane, Ware, and Wilson to stretch for a few measures without him. Frequently Monk would wander backstage, make a phone call, have a chat with the waitresses or the dishwasher, grab a bite to eat, or take a nap while the band played on. Then he would return to the piano and step right back in without missing a beat, as if he had been there all along, listening to every note. Later, Coltrane recalled, "Monk gave me complete freedom. He'd leave the stand for a drink or to do his dance, and I could just improvise by myself for fifteen or twenty minutes before he returned."

Playing with the eccentric genius Monk was a great learning experience for Coltrane. The pianist's approach to music was so unusual for the time that any musician schooled in the traditional jazz forms had to unlearn and relearn many times over as a member of his band. In particular, Coltrane learned new harmonic voicings and ways to play chord progressions. Monk also urged him to experiment with polyphonic tones by developing a technique for playing more than one note at a time, which is very difficult on the saxophone. Still finding his voice and establishing himself in New York, Coltrane was also getting exposure, making connections, and slowly seducing the finicky critics.

Coltrane's wife, Naima, sometimes stopped by the Five Spot with a tape recorder. Then, back at the hotel after a gig, she and her husband would play the tapes back over and over again so that he could study his own improvisations, remembering what he liked and learning from his mistakes. He also listened closely to the other players in the band, trying to get a better feel for their playing styles. The importance of listening closely to other musicians became a creed for Coltrane, who was always searching for new ideas in the playing styles of others.

Six nights a week, from June through December 1957, Coltrane played the Five Spot with Monk, and almost every night, the dark, smoky club was filled beyond capacity with jazz fans. The barriers of age, race, gender, and

Coltrane (left) and Thelonious Monk during the late 1950s. Looking back on his time with Monk, Coltrane called the pianist "a musical architect of the highest order."

class were shattered each night at the Five Spot as people from all walks of life packed into the tiny room. The fans squeezed shoulder-to-shoulder along the bar, crowded around small tables, and lined up along the walls to witness the genius of Thelonious Monk and hear the powerful sheets of sound, the sheer energy, of John Coltrane.

* * *

Nearly ten years later, Coltrane and a friend were in New York and decided to drop in on Monk. They rang the bell of Monk's apartment, and his wife,

Nellie, came to the door. She invited them in, explained that Monk was not home, and sent Thelonious, Jr., to fetch his father, who she suspected was probably chatting with the neighbors. After an hour of waiting, Coltrane and his friend were about to get up and leave when Monk opened the door and let out an ecstatic howl—"Coltrane!" Everyone laughed as the two old friends hugged each other, obviously overjoyed to be reunited.

Then, pointing across the room, Monk said, "Man, I got your picture on my piano. I was just looking at it today!" It was a photograph of John and Naima that had appeared in a Japanese jazz magazine. Out on the terrace, Coltrane turned to Monk and began, "Man, I was just thinking about this music . . ." Then Monk interrupted, "Aw, man . . . You shouldn't think— just play!"

CHAPTER TWO
HIGH POINT

The equinox occurs twice each year, when the sun is directly above the Earth's equator. At these times, day and night are of the same duration, and one season gives way to another. On one such day—September 23, 1926—in Hamlet, North Carolina, summer became fall, and John William Coltrane was born.

John's mother, Alice Blair, was the daughter of Reverend William Wilson Blair, a minister in the African Methodist Episcopal Zion Church in Hamlet. Reverend Blair, who served as a state senator for a time, was a forceful man who loved to give fiery sermons from the pulpit of his church. The church, as was common in many African-American communities, was a center of social and political activity in Hamlet. On Sunday mornings Reverend Blair would often address his congregation about the plight of Southern blacks. He strongly criticized the treatment blacks received from their white neighbors, and he sometimes called on his parishioners to unite in a struggle against racial injustice.

In 1926, Reverend Blair was promoted to presiding elder and was required to preach at various churches throughout the area. So he packed up his family and moved 100 miles to High Point, North Carolina, which was more centrally located within the church district and thus more convenient for his work.

The town of High Point was established in 1859, when the completion of the North Carolina and Midland Railroad made it the highest point on the line between Goldsboro and Charlotte. By the late 1920s, some 35,000 people lived in High Point, about one-third of them African-American. As with most Southern towns of the day, racial segregation in High Point was a way of life sanctioned by law. Black people were expected to step off the sidewalk to make way for whites; to defer to their white counterparts when waiting in line at the general store; to use restrooms and to drink only from water fountains marked "Colored." Black moviegoers had to use separate theater entrances and balconies, and restaurants were divided into white and black sections. Breaking these boundaries was to risk arrest.

Despite the laws and practices that persecuted African-Americans throughout the South, the black community in High Point had maintained its dignity. This was partially because racial segregation was not as strictly enforced in High Point as it was in most other Southern towns, and racial violence was not as common there as elsewhere. Perhaps another reason was that High Point's blacks were religious people with traditional Christian values that united their families and their community. Most of them, particularly those who lived on the south side of town, were laborers, working at menial jobs for little pay, but they were proud people and willing to work hard to get ahead. They valued education, and some of them, especially those who lived on the slightly more upscale east side of town, could realistically hope to send their children to college.

Alice Blair was one member of High Point's black community who had made it to college. Unlike her father, who was outspoken and streetwise, Alice was quiet and thoughtful. She sang and played piano for the gospel choir at church and hoped to be an opera singer. Reverend Blair sent his daughter to Livingston College in Salisbury, North Carolina, where she studied music and education. At Livingston, she met the man who would become her husband and the father of her child. John Robert Coltrane (known as "J. R.") was a tailor from Sanford, North Carolina. He was a quiet and mild-mannered man, with a big smile and a warm personality.

He stood about 5-feet-7-inches, was slim, a sharp dresser, and he loved music. Alice took to him instantly, as he did to her. In 1926, they married and moved into an apartment in Hamlet, where their son, John, was born. Two months later they moved to High Point and moved in with Reverend Blair.

Eight people shared the three-bedroom Blair house: J. R., Alice, and their son, John; Alice's sister, Betty, her husband, Golar Lyerly, and their daughter, Mary; and Reverend Blair and his wife. This happy, tightly knit family was friendly and liked by their neighbors, but because they worked long days, they did not socialize much. J. R. usually worked late

An engraved cornerstone marks John Coltrane's birthplace in Hamlet, North Carolina.

into the evening at a local tailor shop. Within four years of the move to the Blair house, J. R. had his own pressing and cleaning business in High Point, and each evening Alice and John would walk to the shop with J. R.'s supper in hand. After work, J. R. always went straight home to be with the family; he was known throughout the community as a genial, smart, hardworking family man.

When J. R. was not working, he liked to relax with a glass of bourbon whiskey, although he almost never drank more than a glass or two in an evening. And he loved to play music. He often played his ukulele and sang around the house, especially when friends dropped by, and he sometimes played the violin. His favorite song was "The Sweetheart of Sigma Chi," a waltz that had a touching melancholy strain, and he would sing it sweetly but passionately in his full baritone with plenty of vibrato, plucking and strumming, all to the family's utter delight. John especially sat rapt at his father's side as the music filled the house.

As a young boy, John played mostly with his cousin, Mary, with whom he spent countless hours roller-skating. Once he started attending school, however, John spent more time with classmates James Kinzer and Franklin Brower. At school or just kicking around the neighborhoods, the three boys were inseparable. James and Franklin introduced John to baseball, which quickly became John's favorite sport. A good-fielding first baseman who could also hit with power, John and his friends would sometimes wander into other neighborhoods and organize a game with local white boys, even though most adults objected to black and white boys playing on the same field together. John also tried boxing, football, and wrestling. Although he proved to be a natural at every sport he tried, baseball remained one of his passions throughout his life.

The grandson of two ministers, John had an early exposure to religion, and although the Blair house was not a strictly pious one, John did attend Sunday school. He delighted his Sunday school teachers with his seriousness and his intelligent questions, which showed a capacity for understanding beyond his years. He was fascinated by the notion that there was a God or some divine power manifesting in various forms on earth, and he very much wanted to learn more.

Learning was something John did very well. At High Point's Leonard Street Elementary School, he was always at or near the top of his class and performed well on the standardized tests administered by the state. Moreover, John was well liked not only by his peers but also by his teachers. Although in later years he did not do as well in school, he read

The young John Coltrane poses with his third-grade class at the Leonard Street Elementary School in High Point, North Carolina, during the 1934–35 school year.

incessantly, and his unique intelligence was always apparent to those who knew him. While growing up, John had a broad range of interests outside of sports and schoolwork. For example, he liked to read comic books, especially Dick Tracy, Flash Gordon, and Doc Savage. Their heroic efforts in the war on crime stirred his imagination. Automobiles also captured his attention, and he spent many an afternoon chewing on a Baby Ruth and browsing through magazines at the local drugstore, looking for Ford and Chevrolet advertisements. Sometimes he would take pencil and paper and trace the images in the ads; later he developed a good eye and a steady hand and drew his own cars, customizing them to fit his fancy. J. R. often took the family on Saturday jaunts through the countryside, and John loved these outings. Sunday evenings were usually spent at the movies. John also joined the Boy Scouts, and whenever a trip was organized, he was on list to go. John also loved hanging out at Mrs. Drake's Confectionery store in the lobby of the Henley Hotel. The small store had everything a boy could want: candy, soda, ice cream at a nickel a scoop, and lots of magazines. Mrs. Drake almost never threw anyone out for loitering.

Tragedy struck the family when John was twelve years old. J. R., at age thirty-eight, suddenly became seriously ill. He was taken to the hospital, where he died a few days later. The cause of his death remains uncertain. Then, only a few months later, Reverend Blair died, and John's uncle Golar died soon after that. John showed little emotion in response to what must have been a difficult time for him; it would have been like him to want to appear strong for his mother's sake.

After J. R.'s death, John's mother had to earn money, so she went to work as a domestic for local white folks. Many African-American women cooked and cleaned for only three or four dollars a week in those days. When Reverend Blair was alive he would not allow his daughter to do such work, which he considered disgraceful exploitation of black women by whites. But now, with the three male breadwinners in the family dead and buried, there was nobody to protest. Besides, work of any kind was hard to come by in High Point, especially for women—and even more so for black women. Later, John's mother got a job at the local country club that paid better. To help ease the family's financial burden, John worked as a soda jerk for the big-hearted Mrs. Drake during his last two years at High Point's William Penn High School.

John loved to listen to the radio. During the 1930s and 1940s, just about all the music heard over the airwaves was played by white musicians. The big-band sounds of Harry James, the brothers Tommy and Jimmy Dorsey, and Glenn Miller were the order of the day. African-American players were systematically excluded from the airwaves, as well as from recording sessions, some music halls, and the music press, and it was prohibited for a stage band to be racially mixed. To the mainstream jazz media, the emerging black music (and there was plenty of it out there) was too percussive and hard-driving. Once in a while, a daring disk jockey would play some blues or perhaps a song by the cheery Cab Calloway, but black music was rarely heard on the radio. The mostly white jazz critics preferred the more mellow sounds of the big band and swing era, which were more suitable for easy listening, romantic candle-lit suppers, and dancing cheek to cheek. Although the music of the great Duke Ellington and Count Basie occasionally got airplay, John heard little of it on the radio while he was growing up.

Even some members of the black community looked down on the new black jazz, which the older folks called "the devil's music." Gospel, the music of the church, was the most popular music of the African-American community. During Sunday morning services at the St. Stephen's Metropolitan African Methodist Episcopal Zion Church, John got a weekly dose of a rich variety of music—from Bach to Gospel spirituals, sung by an enthusiastic congregation of worshipers. John was moved by all of it. Many of the great singers, musicians, and songwriters in the history of American music trace their roots to the music of the church; John Coltrane was no exception.

The church was not only responsible for John becoming a music lover, it also played a major role in his becoming a musician. One day Reverend

Warren Steele, a preacher at St. Stephen's who was also the Boy Scout troop leader, decided that the black community of High Point needed a band—particularly with the threat of war looming. Though not yet in his teens, John showed up at a meeting in the church basement, eager to sign up.

Before there could be a band, however, there had to be money. To raise the necessary funds, Reverend Steele sent his young would-be musicians door-to-door, armed only with their smiles and their enthusiasm. Though the people of High Point, especially the black people, had very little money to spare, the boys raised enough money to buy about a dozen used instruments. Thus the High Point Community Band was born, and John Coltrane took the first step in what would be a long and fantastic musical journey.

CHAPTER THREE
EARLY TRAINING

*T*he Community Band met every Tuesday evening in the basement of St. Stephen's Church. Reverend Steele, who played the clarinet and had a fairly solid grounding in music theory, showed the boys how to finger the various horns. He taught the budding musicians as a group, but he also showed them how and what to practice on their own.

John started out on alto horn, but one day, when the clarinetist did not come to rehearsal, John asked if he could try the clarinet. He had heard the clarinet playing of Artie Shaw and Woody Herman and liked the sound these skillful players got from the instrument. Reverend Steele had already recognized that John was one of the most talented players in the group, so he agreed to let the boy give the clarinet a blow.

John took the slender black instrument in his hands, placed his fingers on the shiny chrome keys, breathed deeply, closed his lips around the mouthpiece, and filled the room with a deep, woody sound. John played only a few notes, but Reverend Steele was startled by the brilliant tone that surged from the clarinet in the hands of the young Coltrane. Steele realized he was witnessing something very special. The preacher asked John if he could play the passage over again, and John said he would try. With all heads turned in his direction, John repeated the passage, this time embellishing it with some notes from the upper register. The boys looked on with excitement and admiration as Reverend Steele offered John a seat in the band's clarinet section.

John really wanted to play the saxophone. He had been listening to the records of tenor saxophonist Lester Young, who after recording with the Count Basie quintet in 1936 had made a name for himself as a leader. John also admired Johnny Hodges, the outstanding alto saxophonist who performed with Duke Ellington. But neither John nor his mother had the money to buy a horn.

Soon, John met a man named Charlie Haygood, the owner of a local restaurant. When business was slow, Charlie liked to fool around on an alto sax in his kitchen. One day, John heard him playing and stopped in to chat. Eventually, John persuaded Charlie to lend him his horn.

Meanwhile, the Community Band was such a success that Samuel Burford, the principal at William Penn High School, started to form a school band. After the PTA raised enough money to buy a handful of used but serviceable instruments, Burford hired a music teacher from Durham named Grayce Yokley. John was beginning his senior year at William Penn and was by now an outstanding clarinetist in the Community Band. When she arrived in High Point in September 1942, Yokley invited John to occupy the first clarinet chair in the newly formed school band.

Like John, most of the members of the high school band were former Community Band members who had received solid training from Reverend Steele. All of them had good basic knowledge of music theory, could sight-read, and got respectable tone out of their instruments, so John enjoyed the greater challenge as well as the better sound of the new band. John also enjoyed the new band for another reason—young women. Whereas the Community Band was essentially a Boy Scouts group, the high school band was a coeducational enterprise. This made it even more interesting for John.

Even in high school, John had a relatively powerful presence. He was quiet and reserved, even withdrawn, which gave him a certain air of mystery. He had friends, but only a few people knew him well. He was rarely part of large social gatherings. He did, however, attend small parties on weekends. From the money he earned as a soda jerk, John bought himself some sharp clothes, which, combined with his reputation as a budding musician, made him an attractive prospect for young ladies.

John's main interest was a girl named Dorothea Nelson. John's friend Franklin had spotted their attractive young classmate first, but John won her affections. She and John dated for about a year, but after graduation she moved to Washington, D.C., where she took a job with the federal government, thus ending their relationship.

Because the United States was at war during the early 1940s, U.S. industry was engaged in an intensive war effort that created an insatiable demand for labor. Seeing this opportunity to make money, an increasing number of Southerners headed north for New Jersey, New York, Pennsylvania, and other northern states, where there were more factory jobs. John's mother was one of those who migrated north for job opportunities. She arranged to have John stay with relatives and left for New Jersey with her sister.

With his mother away, John socialized more, particularly with young women, sometimes drinking and staying out late. He began to neglect his studies, becoming an average student, rather than the above-average student he had been. But his interest in music never waned; in fact, he now began to spend several hours a day either practicing his clarinet, struggling with Charlie's saxophone, or listening to music.

One day John brought Charlie's alto sax to band practice and impressed his teacher with how well he could play it. In fact, Yokley arranged a song in the band's repertoire, "Tuxedo Junction," to include an alto saxophone solo for John to play. When the band performed the tune onstage, John played the solo beautifully and immediately established himself as the premier player in the group.

John graduated from William Penn High School on May 31, 1943. Because the country was at war, junior-senior proms were low-key affairs. Expenses were kept to a minimum, and the students wore street clothes. At his prom, John was up on the bandstand, playing both clarinet and alto saxophone.

John, Franklin, and James had remained friends throughout high school and graduated together. Then, with their high school diplomas in hand, they decided together to move up north to Philadelphia, Pennsylvania. Franklin's two brothers lived there and had sent word that there was plenty of work in Philadelphia. Also, the three recent graduates knew that as soon as they turned eighteen, they would probably be called to serve in the military. They wanted to have some fun before that day came. They also wanted to continue their education and knew they would need to earn and save a little money for college tuition and living expenses. So on the night of June 11, 1943, high school diplomas in hand, they boarded a train for the City of Brotherly Love.

During the 1940s, Philadelphia was as segregated as most Southern cities were. There were basically two black ghettos—one on the north side of the city, and one on the south side. John, Franklin, and James arrived at the North Philadelphia station and took a taxi to the home of Franklin's brother George, where they set up temporary residence. A few days later, they each found work: James got a job as a grocery clerk, Franklin took a position with the U.S. Signal Corps office, and John landed a job as a laborer at a sugar refinery. Franklin stayed on at his brother's home, and John and James rented a place together—a third-floor apartment on North Twelfth Street.

While he was living in Philadelphia, John stayed in close contact with his family. His mother, who worked in nearby Atlantic City, visited him once or twice a month. For her son's eighteenth birthday, she bought him a used alto sax. In June 1944, John's cousin, Mary, graduated from high school, came to Philadelphia, and moved in with John and James.

While working full-time at the sugar refinery, John enrolled at the Ornstein School of Music on 19th and Spruce streets. He studied saxophone with Mike Guerra, who was, like John, a clarinetist-turned-saxophonist. Guerra had more than twenty years of playing and teaching experience. Guerra said that John "was easily the best student in my class. I wrote out complex chord progressions and special exercises in chromatic scales, and he was one of the few who brought his homework back practically the next day and played it on sight. It was amazing the way he absorbed everything I gave him. He was always asking for more."

After about a year, John left the sugar refinery to work in a Campbell's Soup plant. He also left Ornstein for Granoff Studios, where he received a scholarship to study both the clarinet and the saxophone. Barely into his first year of studies at Granoff, John showed his teachers some music he had written, and he landed a scholarship to study music composition. His teachers were so impressed that a few of them voluntarily gave John three or four extra hours of instruction each week. Often spending ten or twelve hours a day at the school—practicing, composing, studying, and attending classes—John quickly became not only the best student enrolled at Granoff but one of the finest young players ever to attend the school.

John had an extraordinary amount of talent and aptitude, but his progress was not simply the result of natural ability. He was also an extremely devoted young musician who was willing to put in countless hours of hard work. John was motivated by an intense, unwavering desire to be a great musician. Every evening, after a grueling day at school, he returned to his apartment, ate dinner, and got right back to his horn. Each night, without exception, he would practice several hours before going to bed.

John was very methodical in his practice sessions. First he closed himself up in the quiet solitude of his bedroom. Then he opened the case that contained his horn, the shiny brass instrument almost jumping out at him. He selected a reed, carefully trimmed it, and then held it up to the light to make sure it was cut evenly. After securing the reed in the mouthpiece, slowly tightening the two screws that hold it in place, he firmly twisted the mouthpiece into the neck of his horn. Once the horn was ready, John then chose an exercise from his practice book. Only after this ritual was complete did John slide the neck strap over his head, place his long fingers on the keys, bring the mouthpiece to his lips, and begin warming up. And only after playing for several hours would he call it a night and return the tired instrument to its case.

In 1943, James and Franklin were drafted into the military, although Franklin was eventually rejected because of a thyroid condition. John knew it was only a matter of time before he, too, would be called by Uncle Sam. Hoping to put off the draft, John took a civilian job with the Navy Signal Corps, where Franklin, who was now a student at Temple University, used to work. But John was called anyway. In 1945 he was inducted into the U.S. Navy and shipped off to the Hawaiian Islands.

Coltrane (with alto saxophone) takes a break from a U.S. Navy band session in Hawaii in 1946. He was discharged from the Navy that year.

John was not a happy sailor, but he had little reason to complain. After all, while others were going off to possibly die in battle, John was playing clarinet in the Navy marching band. He also played in a dance band called the Melody Masters, which was a big hit on the island of Oahu. When the war ended, John was discharged from the Navy, and in 1946 he returned to his home in the North Side ghetto of Philadelphia.

When John got off the train in Philadelphia, he found the city, and the country, transformed. The war was over, and Americans were busy getting on with their lives. They were spending money and going out more at night, looking for a good time. Dance clubs were thriving, and there was plenty of work for musicians. The swing era seemed to have ended with the war, and black music—particularly rhythm and blues (or R&B, as it was called)—was gaining in popularity. The sweetly lush orchestrations and the romance of the slow dance seemed to fade into history. Now Americans wanted to celebrate their victory in World War II. They needed to jitterbug.

John moved into his old apartment with his friend James, resumed studies with Guerra at Ornstein, and continued his strict practice regimen. Life was much the same as it was before his Navy stint. But now, instead of going to bed after his practice sessions, John began heading out at night to check out the music scene.

About this time, John heard and met an alto saxophonist who was shaking up the world of music, and who would be a powerful influence on John's own playing. The man's friends and adoring fans called him "Yardbird," or simply "Bird," but his real name was Charlie Parker.

CHAPTER FOUR

NOBODY KNOWS . . .

One night, John and his friend Benny Golson, also a saxophonist, went to hear the popular trumpeter Dizzy Gillespie. Gillespie had established himself as one of the finest jazz musicians and bandleaders of the day. Gillespie was known not only for his fine playing but also for his unusual horn, which was bent at a 45-degree angle; his cheeks, which ballooned out when he played; his beret, which he wore dramatically tilted to one side; and his dark glasses, which he frequently looked out over in mock coyness. But the saxophonist in his band, Charlie Parker, had not yet attained the international success he eventually would enjoy. Still, when Parker went into his solos—sometimes growling from a crouched position, sometimes howling with his back arched—the crowd responded to the dynamic, rapid-fire improvisations that surged from the big man's horn. John and Benny had never heard anything like what they were hearing from Parker that night, and the two went backstage after the gig, hoping to catch a glimpse of the man known as Bird.

Charlie Parker was born and raised in Kansas City, Kansas. At the age of eleven, he began playing the alto sax, and by age fifteen, he was going from club to club asking to sit in. When he finally got the chance to flaunt his stuff, at Kansas City's Hi Hat Club, he had the rude awakening that he was not nearly ready to make his debut. He retreated into a regimen of study and practice. He studied harmony with the pianist Carrie Powell and

Alto saxophonist Charlie Parker and trumpeter Dizzy Gillespie—also known to jazz fans as "Bird" and "Diz"—in 1950. Coltrane often mentioned these two bebop titans when discussing his musical influences.

the guitarist Efferge Ware, and he practiced scales and arpeggios for hours at home. He also memorized the solos of the saxophonist Lester Young, his idol, and could eventually play them note for note. In 1937, he took Kansas City's jazz scene by storm, and two years later he moved to New York. There he joined trumpeters Dizzy Gillespie and Roy Eldridge, pianist Thelonious Monk, drummers Max Roach and Kenny Clarke, and guitar legend Charlie Christian to define the bebop era. Charlie Parker transformed the jazz medium with his brilliant technique and improvisational wizardry.

Backstage, the quiet, reserved Coltrane said nothing to the flamboyant Parker. It was not that Coltrane was speechless as much as he seemed content just to be in the presence of such a great musician. But Golson spoke up, asking Bird for his autograph. As he signed for Golson and a long line of other autograph seekers, Parker noticed Coltrane standing quietly off in a corner. They exchanged some words, and Bird asked the young man his name. When the young Coltrane told the older and fairly rotund Parker his name, Bird quipped, "I like your name, my man. It reminds me of a quality brand of English muffins."

After meeting Parker, Coltrane immersed himself in Bird's music, listening to and playing along with his recordings to get a better sense of Bird's methods. From this exercise, Coltrane further developed his technique and gained insight into the limits of the saxophone, and how to push the instrument to those limits. There clearly are similarities between the two players, but a comparison of Parker's recordings with Coltrane's later musical expression yields more differences than similarities. Bird was a melodic improviser, while Coltrane structured his solos on harmonic progression. In other words, Parker's improvisational approach was horizontal, whereas Coltrane's was vertical. Ultimately, the influence of Parker on Coltrane was more inspirational than stylistic, but powerful nonetheless.

By the time he was twenty years old, the dashing John Coltrane of his high school years had been transformed into a somewhat less impressive figure, at least on the surface. He stood about 5 feet 11 inches and weighed 180 pounds, wore dark, loose-fitting clothing, and rarely said anything at all unless he was spoken to—and even then he almost always spoke in soft tones. Oddly, he seldom wore socks or underwear. He almost never went to parties and rarely went out on dates. He was not without a sense of humor, but his mood was usually serious, his eyes downcast. Music was always on his mind, and he seemed to turn away from everything else, not with distaste but with a simple, yet profound, disinterest. In short, there was an intensity to Coltrane that could not be denied, and anyone who came in contact with him was instantly struck by it.

Coltrane went through a difficult period in his early twenties. Although he had steady gigs as a soloist with the Joe Webb Band, he had very little money and had to move into an apartment with his mother, his aunt Betty, and his cousin Mary. It was a small place, so John had only a small section of a room partitioned off for himself. All he owned was a few articles of clothing, a cot to sleep on, a record player, some records, a framed picture of Charlie Parker, and of course, his horn. Alice Coltrane worked as a domestic, Aunt Betty stayed home to do the cooking, and John played day and night, either on his own or with the band.

A big break came in 1947, when John was offered a job by alto saxophonist and bandleader Eddie "Cleanhead" Vinson. Vinson had lost most of his hair by the age of twenty and from then on kept his head clean shaven. He had made his way from Houston, Texas, to Philadelphia, where he hoped to form a band by harvesting some of the city's young talent. When he heard Coltrane rehearsing with pianist Red Garland at the musicians' union hall, Vinson was determined to make John's distinctive sound part of his new band. The only problem, however, was that Vinson played alto, so he needed a tenor saxophonist. He turned to Coltrane and offered to buy him a tenor saxophone if he would make the switch and join the band. Garland, whom Vinson had already hired, urged Coltrane to accept the offer, which he did.

The band toured the country, and Coltrane made the transition from alto to tenor sax nightly before a live audience. At first he disliked the larger instrument, which required more of a stretch from the fingers and a longer column of air out of the lungs, but he grew to appreciate the fuller, deeper voice of the tenor and got used to the difference in feel. Also, Coltrane had become somewhat frustrated with the alto, perhaps because he felt he could never match the mastery of Bird.

While on the road with Vinson, Coltrane met Charlie Parker a second time. During an extended engagement in California in late 1947, Coltrane heard that Bird often showed up at the bassist Red Callender's beach house in the Los Angeles area for impromptu jam sessions. The piano great Erroll Garner was staying with Callender at the time, and drummer Harold West had joined the two of them for a session at the house when Coltrane showed up one afternoon. And there was Bird, playing a slow blues to the beating surf.

That year, Coltrane met Miles Davis, who had played with saxophonists Bird, Coleman Hawkins, and Benny Carter. Coltrane and Miles played together briefly in a quartet, and each expressed a desire to play together again more often.

The Vinson band broke up in mid-1948 after their tour ended, and Coltrane continued to give the tenor sax the same attention as he did the alto. And with the new instrument came a whole new world of influences— Coleman Hawkins, Ben Webster, and Jimmy Oliver, whom Coltrane had heard perform but who never made any recordings. Coltrane had enjoyed playing with Vinson and had learned a lot, but touring was difficult for him. While on the road, he rarely ate a balanced meal, drank lots of bourbon, smoked two packs of cigarettes a day, and frequently indulged his peculiar weakness—sweet-potato pie. So he was glad to get off the tour circuit for a while.

Out of work, Coltrane set about looking for a new gig. He briefly hooked up with trumpeter Mel Melvin and the Heath brothers—drummer Al, bassist Percy, and alto saxophonist Jimmy. Later that year, 1948, the Heaths formed their own band and invited Coltrane to join the group as a second alto player. He accepted the offer but continued to play with numerous other musicians, including trumpeter Calvin Massey, nicknamed "Folks," who would become one of John's closest friends. After a gig with trumpeter and bandleader

Although Coltrane started his saxophone study on alto and later mastered soprano saxophone, his main instrument was tenor sax (pictured). The tenor and alto sax look similar, but the tenor can be distinguished by its larger size and curved neck.

Howard McGhee at New York's famed Apollo Theater, Coltrane received his first public review, a positive one in the Philadelphia *Tribune*. But when the band went on to play gigs in Chicago, McGhee replaced Coltrane with Jimmy Heath, and John was once again in search of work.

A string of one-time, $10-a-night gigs followed. Coltrane grew restless playing clubs where he had trouble hearing himself over the loud conversation and the crashing of dishes and glasses. Knowing that the audience was only half-listening, Coltrane began to experiment onstage, and club owners started criticizing his music as too far out of the mainstream. For them, the integrity of the music was not enough. They wanted him to entertain the drunken crowds with silly gimmicks—jump up on the bar and strut while honking on his horn. Around this time, a depressed Coltrane began using drugs.

Although drugs were commonplace in the jazz community, so was religion, and many musicians have been saved from self-destruction by finding God in some form or another. During the mid-1940s, the religion of Islam gained acceptance among black musicians such as Art Blakey, Yusef Lateef, Ahmad Jamal, and Talib Daoud. When Daoud, a drummer, moved to Philadelphia in 1947, he did much to bring the Islamic religion to musicians there. Coltrane, a relatively devout Christian, began to discuss religion with friends and other musicians.

Coltrane was reunited with Jimmy Heath in 1949, when the two of them joined a band led by Dizzy Gillespie. Coltrane made his first recordings with this band, on the Capitol label, in New York on November 21 of that year. The band toured the country and enjoyed great success, but Coltrane continued to drink lots of whiskey and take drugs. Eventually he had to be reprimanded for not showing up at a gig because he was drunk.

Some of the other members of the band tried to lead Coltrane away from his self-abusive habits. For instance, the tenor player Yusef Lateef, who was briefly with the band, had read a lot of Eastern philosophy and had converted to Islam. He took an immediate liking to Coltrane and recommended he try reading the philosophers Kahlil Gibran and Krishnamurti, whose writings had greatly changed Lateef's life. Another band member,

Bill Barron, gave him a book on yoga. All of this seemed a bit esoteric to the good Christian boy from High Point, North Carolina, but Coltrane was open-minded and he read the literature.

After Coltrane joined a band led by alto player Earl Bostic, the band went into the recording studio on two occasions. The first time was in Cincinnati, Ohio, on April 7, 1952; the other was in Los Angeles, California, on August 15 of the same year. Later that year, Coltrane made a record in Nashville, Tennessee, with the Gay Crosse band. Crosse, a tenor saxophonist and vocalist, mixed R&B with comic routines and drew large crowds. When he returned to Philadelphia, Coltrane joined another R&B group—Daisy Mae and the Hepcats. Daisy Mae would strut out in a shimmering tight dress, while her husband played boogie-woogie guitar behind her. R&B put much-needed money in Coltrane's pockets, but he found little artistic satisfaction in playing the gigs with Crosse and Daisy Mae. He fell into a period of deep depression.

Countless explanations have been offered as to why so many musicians have abused alcohol and other dangerous drugs. Some players have claimed that certain drugs heighten awareness and sensitivity and free up the creative process; others believe that drugs merely give the illusion that a performance is better than without them. Still others point out that poor people with little hope of improving their lives often turn to drugs, and that since most jazz musicians struggle just to get by, they are naturally susceptible to the temptations of getting high. Ultimately, there is no single reason why people take drugs, but most musicians—and most writers and artists as well—would probably agree that a person with alcohol or drug problems is less likely to achieve his or her goals, no matter what the field of endeavor. During the early 1950s (probably in 1953), for whatever reason, Coltrane started shooting heroin.

Fortunately for him, Coltrane met a woman in 1953 who would help him get through this troubled time. Her name was Naima. It was a hot night in July when Naima and John met at the home of a mutual friend, bassist Steve Davis. They left together for a walk in the park and wound up spending the entire night walking and talking together. He told her about his drug habit and how he was trying to kick it. They talked about religion, music, and relationships, and they listened closely to each other as they shared their most personal thoughts.

Born in Philadelphia, Naima, whose Christian name was Juanita, was a converted Muslim, meaning she had become a follower of Islam. When she met Coltrane, she was working as a seamstress in a factory, supporting herself and her five-year-old daughter, Antonia (later called by her Muslim name, Saeeda). She had never married and was sharing a house with her brother and his wife. Naima was interested in astrology and was pleased that John was a Virgo, a sign compatible with hers, which was Capricorn. Naima also loved music, especially jazz, and although she often went to jazz clubs, she had never heard John play before they met. John found that he could overcome his shyness with Naima, and she found John's gentle demeanor to be something very special. He introduced her to his family, and soon their relationship started to become more intimate.

A month after they met, John invited Naima to a gig so that she could hear him play. A month after that, John told her in a very matter-of-fact way that they would be married. When she asked him how he knew that when he had not even asked her to be his wife, he simply responded by proposing to her. The same year that John met Naima, he joined a band led by the alto saxophonist Johnny Hodges. Hodges, who rose to prominence while working with Duke Ellington, was the most important alto saxophone stylist before Charlie Parker. When Hodges went off to start his own band, he invited Coltrane to play tenor. Coltrane jumped at the chance to play with his childhood idol.

Playing with Hodges, Coltrane learned a great deal, particularly about intonation. While Hodges was soloing, Coltrane watched from the side of the stage, moved by the power of the Hodges sound. That sound was in stark contrast with that of Parker: While Bird had speed and embellished each solo with dynamic melodic bursts, Hodges caressed each passing phrase, holding onto each note until he had to let go. When Coltrane moved

Saxophonist Johnny Hodges, known for his work with the Duke Ellington band, was an important influence on the young John Coltrane.

into the spotlight to solo on, for example, "Smoke Gets in Your Eyes," he extended some of his lines, clearly taking a lesson from Hodges, but always focusing on harmonic development, as was his style.

The band toured with the singer Billy Eckstine, and Coltrane earned $250 a week, well above average for a musician in those days. Benny Golson joined the tour and roomed with his old friend John. But in September 1954, Hodges had to ask Coltrane to leave the band because his drug habit was getting in the way of the music.

Coltrane returned to Philadelphia worked with an assortment of local bands. He continued to use drugs and to drink excessively. He had long neglected caring for his teeth, and they were getting progressively worse, often causing him intense pain during his solos. The drinking and drugs also caused stomach problems, but still he continued to put on weight. Coltrane

During the 1950s, John Coltrane lived in this Philadelphia house on North 33rd Street with his first wife, Naima, and her daughter, Antonia (also known by her Muslim name, Saeeda).

got plenty of work and played with such outstanding players as the tenor saxophonist Odean Pope, then only a teenager, the organist Jimmy Smith, and the percussionist Bill Carney. Sometimes a gig would require that he go to New York, where he played with the pianist Billy Taylor. He continued to work, but now more than ever, Coltrane was struggling under the burden of his drug habit.

In March 1955, Coltrane heard the sad news that Charlie Parker was dead. Had he not destroyed himself with drugs and alcohol for most of his adult life, Parker could have given the world so much more music. He was only thirty-four years old when he died. A doctor who was unaware of Parker's age examined his body on the day of his death and estimated that the saxophonist was in his fifties.

Coltrane took Parker's early death as a warning and struggled even harder to shake his own drug habit. He and Naima were married on October 3, 1955, and the family of three—John, Naima, and Saeeda—moved in with John's mother. Also that year, Coltrane formed a union with another soulmate, Miles Davis.

CHAPTER FIVE
STRAIGHT, NO CHASER

*M*iles Davis was an enigmatic figure who would change musical direction continually. The son of a dentist, Miles had not only the talent but also the money to attend New York's prestigious Juilliard School of Music. His stint at Juilliard was brief, however, as he dropped out to immerse himself in the city's jazz scene and play with Charlie Parker. He made his mark on New York's jazz scene from the moment he walked onstage, playing in the muted, minimalist style that became his signature. Very soon after making his debut with Parker, Miles formed his own band, always skimming off the cream of the current crop of young jazz musicians.

The Philadelphia drummer "Philly" Joe Jones recommended John Coltrane—or "Trainee," as most people by now referred to him—to Miles Davis in 1955. Miles was forming a quintet and wanted a tenor player. He had played with Coltrane before and ever since wanted to get together with him again. Miles told Joe to invite John to join the new band for a gig in Baltimore, and Coltrane accepted the invitation. The new band consisted of Joe Jones on drums, Red Garland on piano, Paul Chambers (then only nineteen years old) on bass, Coltrane on tenor, and of course, Miles on trumpet.

Miles had a unique way of leading the band. He constantly encouraged his musicians to explore new territory, to push their instruments—and

Miles Davis

themselves—to the limit without fear of falling out of time or missing a note. As a result, the music would sometimes start to spin out of control. At that point, Miles would step in, play just the right phrase through his muted horn, and subtly put the group back on course. There were few rehearsals, so the musicians had to listen very closely to each other on stage.

Trane's free-wheeling, harmonic style of playing was well suited to the Miles Davis Quintet. Miles's emphasis on individual exploration allowed Trane to experiment, which is what he most loved to do. Often during a number Miles would leave the bandstand for long stretches, giving the other band members time to develop elaborate solos. Each player had virtually unlimited space in which to create and develop.

Very soon after the group was formed, Miles had the musicians in the recording studio. Their first album, entitled *The New Miles Davis Quintet*, was recorded on October 27, 1955, on the Prestige label. The writer Nat Hentoff, then working as a jazz critic, reviewed the album in the May 16, 1956, issue of *Down Beat* magazine. He praised all the musicians in the group but wrote that Coltrane's playing lacked originality and described his solos as a "mixture of Dexter Gordon, Sonny Rollins, and Sonny Stit." This kind of criticism was typical of jazz critics of the day. Many either did not understand what Coltrane was trying to do or simply preferred a more traditional playing style. And Coltrane's playing was anything but traditional.

One night the band played at the Cafe Bohemia in New York, and Coltrane showed up for the gig strung out on drugs, a disheveled mess. He could barely keep his balance onstage, and his solos went nowhere. Miles, who had kicked his own drug habit in 1954 and was now clean, had a certain tolerance for his musicians using drugs and alcohol, but not when it interfered with the music. Coltrane's drug habit continued to eat at him, body and soul, and it has been said that Miles gave his tenor player an ultimatum: Clean up or get out!

Coltrane returned to the recording studio in September 1956, to team up with Chambers on an album under the latter's name. Two Coltrane original songs—"Nita" and "Just For Love"—appeared on the record. Then, on October 26, Miles brought the quintet back into the studio to record another album for Prestige.

When Coltrane showed no signs of kicking his drug habit, Miles reformed the quintet with Sonny Rollins on tenor instead of Coltrane. John was despondent when he got the news that Sonny was in and he was out. Naima tried to console him by suggesting he form his own group. Coltrane had wanted to lead his own band ever since he had worked with Johnny Hodges, and now was as good a time as any. But first, he knew that he had to get clean—no more drugs, including alcohol and cigarettes.

Coltrane went to the Red Rooster on 52nd Street in New York to hear a group led by his old friend, trumpet player Calvin Massey. Alto saxophonist Clarence Sharpe, drummer Al "Tutti" Heath, and bassist Jimmy Garrison were in the band, along with pianist McCoy Tyner, then an unknown. Massey introduced Coltrane to Tyner, and the two quickly hit it off. Coltrane also met the club owner, who promptly invited him to bring in a group of his own, which he agreed to do.

In the early spring of 1957, Coltrane invited Tyner, Garrison, and Heath to join him and trumpet player Johnnie Splawn for a series of nights at the Rooster. Thus Coltrane made his debut as a leader. The week got off to a shaky start, but once the musicians got to know each other better, the music began to flow. Then, one night, having gone "cold turkey" only weeks before, Coltrane experienced withdrawal symptoms that were so intense he had to leave the bandstand.

Unable to finish the engagement at the Rooster, Coltrane spent three days at home. His body trembled in a cold sweat, and his words were unintelligible. When he was able, he prayed. He knew that a dose of heroin would relieve the pain, but he was determined to free himself from his addictions. The agony continued, and Naima feared her husband would not make it. Coltrane locked himself in his bedroom, leaving only to go to the bathroom, and Naima could hear him groaning and sobbing, day and night. About a week later, when the pain finally subsided, Trane knew it was over. He could return to the living. Suddenly he awoke to a deeper, more spiritual vision of his life and his music.

Coltrane wanted to take his playing to a new level, to break out of his old ways and free his playing from all that was cliché. He was tired of hearing that he sounded like Johnny Hodges, Lester Young, and Dexter Gordon. He was determined to establish his own sound, his own voice. He wanted his audience to say other horn players sounded like him, not that he sounded like others.

With his addictions behind him and his goals clearly defined, Coltrane got right to work, immersing himself in a practice regimen that was even more rigorous than the one he had followed in his younger days.

He started early each morning, practiced all day, and received few visitors. His method was to isolate certain elements of his playing, such as tones, scales, chords, and harmony, and set aside a definite amount of time for practicing each element. When he saw that the hard work was paying off in real technical advancement and a noticeable improvement in his tone, he was encouraged to work even harder.

When he was not practicing, Coltrane saw a lot of his friend and fellow saxophonist, Odean Pope. The two shared their ideas about how to practice and urged each other on in the pursuit of musical excellence. Coltrane associated with other musicians as well during this time. John Glenn, for example, a tenor player who was also skilled at horn maintenance and repair, showed Trane a technique for playing more than one note at a time. Coltrane practiced this technique relentlessly and eventually mastered it. McCoy Tyner also stopped by frequently to chat and offer his support.

More than anything now, Coltrane wanted to put his own group together and land a recording contract. With his short-lived and ill-fated first effort as a leader behind him, he was now confident he could make it work. And he needed a recording deal because he and Naima needed the money.

Coltrane was back in the studio recording for Prestige on March 22, 1957. The album, *Interplay for Two Trumpets and Two Tenors,* showcased the talents of trumpeters Webster Young and Idrees Sulieman and saxophonists Bobby Jaspar and Coltrane. Other players on the album included guitarist Kenny Burrell, pianist Mal Waldron, bassist Paul Chambers, and drummer Arthur Taylor. On this record, the jazz world was offered a glimpse of the new John Coltrane, and those who caught that glimpse were excited by the great music it promised.

Later that March, Coltrane got his contract. He was offered a deal by Prestige that included a $300 advance on each album. It wasn't much money, but Coltrane signed nonetheless, with an option that would leave him free to record for other labels with certain limitations.

Three weeks later, the ink on the Prestige contract barely dry, Coltrane was back in the studio recording for the Riverside label as a guest artist on a Thelonious Monk album. Monk and Riverside had conceived the album as a solo piano venture, but as the project unfolded, the pianist decided he wanted to record the tune "Monk's Mood" as a duet with Coltrane. He convinced his producer to invite Coltrane to appear on the album. Also that April, Coltrane recorded with friends Kenny Burrell, Mal Waldron, and Arthur Taylor, as well as the baritone saxophonist Cecil Payne and drummer Doug Watkins. In May of that year, John and Naima decided that if he was going to get his music heard, New York was where they had to go. New York City was the center of the jazz world. Record companies, jazz clubs, the press, and thousands of talented musicians, including Miles Davis, were located there. Toward the end of the month, John took a train to New York, and Naima agreed to join him later. He stayed for a while at the Alvin Hotel on 52nd Street in Manhattan.

Coltrane was swept up by the city's jazz scene as soon as he arrived in New York. Only days after he got there, he recorded his first album under his own name, *The First Train*. For the session, he was joined by Johnny Splawn on trumpet, Sahib Shihab on baritone saxophone, Red Garland on piano, Paul Chambers on bass, and Al Heath on drums. Then, in mid-June, he played a gig with a quartet led by Monk at a club called the Five Spot in Manhattan.

Born in 1920, the pianist/composer Thelonious Sphere Monk was, like Coltrane, a North Carolina native. As a child, Monk's parents brought him to New York, where he grew up. He began studying the piano at the age of 11, but he was essentially self-taught, figuring things out while playing in local bands. His early work was with the guitarist Charlie Christian and Dizzy Gillespie, and later he recorded mostly as a solo pianist. Several of his compositions, such as "Blue Monk" and "Round About Midnight," are jazz classics and have remained a challenge for every jazz pianist after him. His unorthodox technique, angular rhythmic sense, and reclusive nature placed Monk somewhat on the fringe of the jazz world, but his appearances always drew large crowds, and his records consistently sold well. Coltrane had this to say about the experience of playing with the "High Priest of Bop":

Thelonious Monk. Coltrane's late-1950s performances with Monk at the Manhattan jazz club the Five Spot are legendary.

Working with Monk brought me close to a musical architect of the highest order. I felt I learned from him in every way through the senses, theoretically, technically. I would talk to Monk about musical problems, and he would sit at the piano and show me the answers just by playing them. . . . I think Monk is one of the true greats of all time. He's a real musical thinker—there's not many like him. I feel myself fortunate to have had the opportunity to work with him. If a guy needs a little spark, a boost, he can just be around Monk, and Monk will give it to him.

After Naima and her daughter joined John in New York, they stayed with Paul Chambers at his Brooklyn apartment while looking for a place of their own. Then they moved into a small Manhattan apartment near Central Park West. The apartment was furnished, but barely, and they had little money to spend on anything but food.

John practiced by day and played at the Five Spot by night. On his rare days off, he sometimes played gigs in Washington, D.C. He also continued to record. On September 15, 1957, he went into the studio to do an album for Blue Note Records with trumpeter Lee Morgan, trombonist Curtis Fuller, pianist Kenny Drew, and his old buddies Paul Chambers and Joe Jones. The album was entitled *Blue Train*.

The late 1950s was a period of great transformation for jazz. Much of its traditions and influences—blues, gospel, and African rhythms—were still apparent in the music, but a few innovative musicians, such as saxophonist Ornette Coleman and pianists Cecil Taylor and Sun Ra, were creating sounds that critics and audiences were having trouble grasping. They were leading a movement to push the music into the future, to some extent by returning it to its African roots, and the complexities of their compositions were unprecedented in the short history of jazz. Coltrane's music was central in this movement, and during the next decade he would astound everyone who heard him.

CHAPTER SIX
MILES AHEAD

By the end of 1957, Coltrane was back with Miles Davis, who this time had organized a sextet. The personnel included Julian "Cannonball" Adderley on alto sax, Coltrane on tenor, either Wynton Kelly or Bill Evans on piano, either Philly Joe Jones or Jimmy Cobb on drums, Paul Chambers on bass, and Miles.

In forming the new group, Miles not only surrounded himself with some new personalities, but he also changed his approach to the music. Miles's new compositions had fewer chord changes, the result of a conscious decision to allow the improvisers more room to move, both vertically on the chord and horizontally from one chord to the next. Coltrane thrived in the new setting, stimulated by the fresh talent in the group and enjoying the freedom Miles was granting his players with his new compositions.

As happy as he was at being reunited with Miles, Coltrane continued to record under his own name. On February 7, 1958, he recorded *Soultrane* with drummer Arthur Taylor, bassist Paul Chambers, and pianist Red Garland. He also recorded with a band led by pianist George Russell.

Coltrane was now well known throughout the jazz world, mostly because of the exposure he received as a member of the Miles Davis Sextet, but critics continued to have a hard time appreciating his work. For example, on July 3, 1958, the Miles Davis Sextet traveled to Rhode Island and

One of the all-time greatest small jazz ensembles featured (from left): Bill Evans (piano), Jimmy Cobb (drums), Paul Chambers (bass), Davis (trumpet), and Coltrane (tenor sax). The group is pictured here at the Newport Jazz Festival in 1958.

played the Newport Jazz Festival, one of the top jazz festivals in the world. A review in *Down Beat* magazine called the performance "more confusing to listeners than educational." The reviewer specifically criticized Coltrane's playing as "motion without progress." Coltrane was miles ahead of most of the critics, and it would be some time before they would catch up with him.

On the other hand, audiences and some critics were hearing and appreciating what Coltrane was doing. One day, Coltrane received a letter from a fan who had also enclosed an article from a Cleveland, Ohio, newspaper. The article listed the top 20 jazz albums of 1957. Three albums Coltrane had recorded under his own name were on the list, and he appeared as a sideman on two other albums. The International Critics Poll ranked Coltrane second in the "new star" category, behind Benny Golson, and he placed among the top saxophone players in numerous other polls.

Coltrane still wanted to form a band of his own, and playing with various musicians was a way to get to know the players around the scene. In January 1959, he brought together tenor saxophonist Wayne Shorter, trumpeter Freddie Hubbard, bassist George Tucker, and drummer Elvin Jones for a gig at a New York nightspot. Tommy Flannagan and Cedar Walton took turns at the piano. The music was astounding, convincing Coltrane that the time was right to put together a group of his own. He proposed the idea to Naima, who suggested he wait until after the upcoming tour with Miles, which would give him added exposure that could help him launch his career as a leader. John knew she was right and agreed to wait until the tour was over.

In May, Coltrane went into the studio and recorded *Giant Steps*, to this day an essential album in any jazz collection. The album is a presentation of musical portraits inspired by Coltrane's friends and family; two of the songs—"Naima" and "Cousin Mary"—are actually named after family members. Having left Prestige, Coltrane recorded *Giant Steps* for the Atlantic label, which released it in 1960. The other players on the session were Tommy Flannagan, Arthur Taylor, and Paul Chambers. (The tune "Mr. P. C." was named after Chambers.)

The Miles Davis Sextet went on tour and received glowing reviews, and now some critics, although not as eager to praise Coltrane as they were to praise Miles, were beginning to appreciate Coltrane's playing. For instance, in a detailed and excellent analysis of Coltrane's musicianship, the music critic Zita Carno wrote the following in the October and November 1959 issues of *Jazz Review* magazine:

His command of the instrument is almost unbelievable. Tempos don't faze him in the least; his control enables him to handle a very slow ballad without having to resort to the double-timing so common among hard blowers, and for him there is no such thing as too fast a tempo. His playing is very clean and accurate, and he almost never misses a note. His range is something to marvel at. . . . He is very subtle, often deceptive—but he's always right there. . . . Coltrane the instrumentalist—powerful, sensitive, ahead, and always experimenting.

Nat Hentoff, then an editor and critic for *Jazz Review,* also began to appreciate Coltrane's music. In the liner notes to *Giant Steps*, Hentoff, who earlier had been unsure about Coltrane's experimental style, wrote the following during the late 1950s:

What makes Coltrane one of the most interesting players is that he's not apt to ever stop looking for ways to perfect what he's already developed and also to go beyond what he knows he can do. He is thoroughly involved with plunging as far into himself and the expressive possibilities of his horn as he can. . . . [O]ne quality that can always be expected from Coltrane is intensity. He asks so much of himself that he can thereby bring a great deal to the listener who is also willing to try relatively unexplored territory with him.

But Coltrane was still a long way from receiving wide critical acclaim. For example, the critic Whitney Balliett wrote in *The New Yorker* that "Coltrane's tone is harsh, flat, querulous, and at times almost vindictive. . . . His tone is bleaker than need be, many of his notes are useless, and his rhythmic methods are frequently just clothes flung all over a room." But even after making these criticisms, Balliett went on to write that "despite his blatancy, Trane is an inventive, impassioned improviser who above all traps the listener with the unexpected."

Yet another critic, Charles Hanna, was extremely positive, writing the following in the Minneapolis *Sunday Tribune*:

Coltrane's had something important to say for a long time, but only recently has he found a suitable way of expressing himself. . . . He plays a chord five different ways, milking every possible sound from its structure. He avoids the dangers of a clinical sound with use of a good rhythmic sense and a deeply emotional tone. . . . Coltrane has found his way.

Giant Steps *(album cover)*

Coltrane met Sun Ra late in 1959, and they immediately recognized each other as kindred spirits. Growing up poor in Alabama, Sun Ra was a child prodigy who, with virtually no musical training, could sight-read music and play the piano brilliantly when he was only seven years old. As a teenager he played club dates, but his extremely unorthodox musical sense and tastes often alienated him not only from his audience but from other musicians as well. Later in his career, he constantly brought together outstanding young players fresh out of Juilliard or some other prestigious music school to play in his band, which he called "the arkestra" and usually included about twenty musicians. Onstage, he wore outrageous costumes, including a sparkling metal skullcap, brightly colored robes, boldly printed shirts, furs, beads, and bells. One night Sun Ra played some of his recorded tapes for Coltrane and explained what he was trying to do. Coltrane not only understood the music immediately but soon gained a unique appreciation of Sun Ra's extraordinary musical mind, and the two became friends.

The alto saxophonist Ornette Coleman, a Texan, another musician experimenting on the fringe of the jazz world, struck up a friendship with John Coltrane. A mostly self-taught player and composer, Coleman developed a complex theory of musical improvisation, which he called the harmolodic method, that diverged from the traditional chord-based forms. In 1959 he formed a quartet with bassist Charlie Haden, drummer Billy Higgins, and trumpeter Don Cherry, which made its debut at the Five Spot. Typically audiences would come away from Coleman's performances both dazed and inspired, muttering "I think he's great, but I have no idea what he's doing" or "I don't know where he's going, but it's definitely the future."

George Russell, a pianist with whom Coltrane had recorded the year before, was another musician assaulting the traditions of Western music. He formed his own theory of composition and improvisation, which he explained in a book, *The Lydian Chromatic Concept of Tonal Organization*. In late 1959, Coltrane and Ornette Coleman went to visit Russell to share some ideas. Coleman and Russell each had his own distinct approach to making music, and both were doing things that were very different from what Coltrane was doing at the time. But Coltrane, always searching, believed it was important for him to look at musical perspectives other than his own.

Part of his searching included an exploration into religion and philosophy, prompted, to some extent, by his reading *On and By Krishnamurti* and *Krishnamurti's Commentaries on Living*. Coltrane had borrowed these books from Bill Evans. Coltrane read other books as well, delving into various subject areas, including Eastern religions, Western philosophy, astrology, scientology, yoga, art, the physical sciences, and African history. He read the works of Edgar Cayce, Kahlil Gibran, Plato, Aristotle, and Einstein. As his personal library grew, so did his musical library, which now included recordings of not only Western music but also music from Africa, Afghanistan, India, and other countries. Increasingly in 1959, Coltrane's solos reflected these varied intellectual, spiritual, and ethnic influences.

That year, the Miles Davis Sextet recorded the classic *Kind of Blue*, one of the great jazz recordings of all time and probably the best first purchase on which to build a jazz collection. Against all convention, Miles decided on the pieces to be included on *Kind of Blue* very shortly before the recording sessions took place, so the musicians had no time to study the music or to prepare their solos in advance. Usually, the musicians scheduled to play on a record are given musical charts ahead of time, and they go through a number of rehearsals before recording in the studio. Jazz musicians are often expected to improvise extensively at recording sessions, but usually they have some idea of what will be expected of them before arriving at the studio. For *Kind of Blue*, the players came into the studio with no charts, no rehearsals, and therefore no idea of what Miles had in mind. This was precisely what Miles wanted. He wanted to record an album of pure jazz, one that was spontaneous, with solos improvised entirely on the spot.

The tunes on the album are musical pictures that drift into one another to form a broad tonal landscape of pastel moods, clearly reflecting Miles's

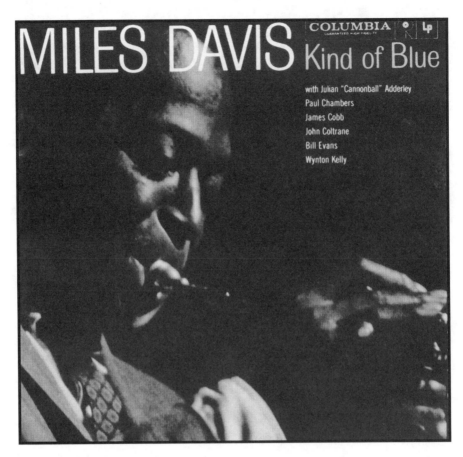

Kind of Blue *(album cover)*

new approach to the music. Each piece is no more than a simple, delicately structured framework, and the musicians build on each one in masterfully subtle ways. The musical setting of *Kind of Blue* is described best by Bill Evans, who played piano on all but one of the pieces and wrote the following in the album's liner notes:

> *There is a Japanese visual art in which the artist is forced to be spontaneous. He must paint on a thin stretched parchment with a special*

brush and black water paint in such a way that an unnatural or
interrupted stroke will destroy the line or break through the parchment.
Erasures or changes are impossible. These artists must practice a
particular discipline, that of allowing the idea to express itself in
communication with their hands in such a direct way that deliberation
cannot interfere.

The resulting pictures lack the complex composition and textures of ordinary painting, but it is said that those who see well find something in them that escapes explanation.

As the painter needs his framework of parchment, the improvising musical group needs its framework in time. Miles Davis presents frameworks here that are exquisite in their simplicity and yet contain all that is necessary to stimulate performance with a sure reference to the primary conception.

The improvisational freedom this music gave the musicians was well suited to Coltrane's playing at the time. But he was quickly growing restless with the sextet. Now, more than ever, he was anxious to form his own group, perform his own compositions and arrangements, and record consistently under his own name. Moreover, the multicultural influences on which Coltrane was now drawing increasingly cut against the grain of Miles's delicate brushstrokes. The angry young tenor, as some critics now referred to Coltrane, was ready to cut loose and follow his own muse.

A few days before Christmas, the Coltranes moved out of Manhattan and into a two-story, three-bedroom brick house with a yard in the St. Albans section of Queens, New York. Unfortunately, John could not relax and enjoy the holidays with Naima and Saeeda; he had to leave almost immediately for Chicago to play a gig with Miles. But when he returned, he found that Naima had turned the house into a home, having bought furniture and a piano. Most welcoming upon his return home was the smell of home-baked sweet-potato pie.

Coltrane's bad eating habits, particularly his endless quest to satisfy his appetite for sweets, affected his weight, his teeth, and his playing.

John in a pensive moment in a recording studio

When his persistent weight problem got out of control, which it frequently did, Coltrane would try to tame his appetite by sucking on butter rum Life Savers, which he always kept in his pockets. He also went on crash diets, after which he would promptly gain back all the weight he had lost. He tried health-food diets too, eating only organically grown fruits and vegetables, only to return eventually to his junk-food binges.

Over the years, Coltrane's bad eating habits had ruined his teeth, and now their deteriorating state sometimes made playing the saxophone quite painful. In fact, there were times when his toothaches were so bad onstage that he had to lay out for a number, or even for an entire set. Finally a dentist told Coltrane that if he did not have major dental work done soon, he would not be able to play the saxophone at all. Coltrane then had most of his teeth shaved down and capped.

These struggles aside, the Coltrane house was a hive of activity in the early 1960s. Musicians dropped by constantly, sometimes merely to sit and exchange ideas over coffee and other times arriving with instruments in hand for an impromptu jam session. In addition, Coltrane began studying and practicing yoga, often in front of the television, which he usually tuned in to a baseball game or a movie. He also loved to drive his 1958 Plymouth and later his Mercury and Chrysler station wagons. Sometimes he would bring "toys" home for the family. Once he brought home a harp for Naima and urged her to learn to play it; another time it was a telescope. On clear nights John, Naima, and Saeeda would gaze through the telescope for hours, awed by the majesty of the heavens. For the Coltranes, the future promised a wealth of love and creativity; it was in the stars.

CHAPTER SEVEN
CIVIL DISOBEDIENCE

*W*hen the Miles Davis Sextet returned from its European tour in 1960, Coltrane gave Davis two-weeks notice that he was leaving the group. The main reason for his deciding to leave was that the Davis sextet had become too constraining for Coltrane. Now, more than ever, he wanted to break into some very new musical territory of his own. Also, the recent success of *Giant Steps* gave him the confidence and the recognition on which to build a career as a bandleader.

When word got around that he was going out on his own, Coltrane was approached by several club owners who wanted to line up engagements. After weighing his many options, he lined up a nine-week stint at the Jazz Gallery, a New York club owned by the same people who owned the Five Spot, where he had played with Monk and others.

Coltrane then set about forming a band. He started with his old friend, the bassist Steve Davis, who had introduced him to Naima. Once Davis agreed to join, Coltrane turned to the question of a pianist. His first choice on piano was McCoy Tyner, but Tyner was playing in Benny Golson's band at the time and was not willing to go back on his prior commitment. So when pianist Steve Kuhn, a twenty-two-year-old Harvard graduate, contacted him about a job, Coltrane decided to give him a try. They met in a rehearsal studio, played together, and two days later Coltrane gave Kuhn the job. Then Coltrane thought about a drummer. His first choice was Elvin Jones, but

The John Coltrane Quartet performs in Indianapolis, Indiana, in 1962. The group included (from left) McCoy Tyner, Coltrane, Jimmy Garrison, and Elvin Jones.

Jones was in jail doing time for a drug conviction. So Coltrane sought advice from Sonny Rollins, who quickly recommended drummer Pete LaRoca. He, too, had a previous commitment to another band, but unlike Tyner, LaRoca broke it in order to play with Coltrane. Thus the John Coltrane Quartet was born.

Entering the Jazz Gallery on the night of the debut of the John Coltrane Quartet in May 1960, one felt the excitement running through the crowd—a group of actors, writers, students, critics, jazz purists, beatniks, politicos, poseurs, and of course, musicians. There were familiar faces too—the avant-garde pianist Cecil Taylor was in the balcony, and Monk was down in front.

When the group walked onstage and jumped into the first tune, Coltrane was nervous, and this affected the performance. But as soon as he got comfortable, Coltrane had the crowd mesmerized, eventually whipping them into a frenzy with a blistering solo. Some stood and chanted his name over and over again. Monk danced in the aisles. The strong rhythm section firmly in the groove, Coltrane carried his audience higher and higher until everyone was convulsing to the beat.

After the show, Coltrane graciously smiled and thanked the audience, many of whom tried to reach out and touch him as he stepped off the bandstand. The debut was an overwhelming success, and the weeks that followed fulfilled all the promise of the first night. Sonny Rollins having stepped out of the scene for a time, there was now only one man to watch on tenor saxophone—John Coltrane.

The critics reeled with enthusiasm, but Coltrane was not satisfied. Several weeks after the group's auspicious debut, he decided to make a change. One night after a gig, Coltrane approached Steve Kuhn, put his arm around him, and said, "There's some things I want to hear that you're not doing." Whatever those things were, Coltrane believed that McCoy Tyner was the pianist who could do them. He extended the invitation, and Tyner, who was now looking for work, accepted and finished the stint at the Jazz Gallery.

Tyner was clearly more suited to the group than Kuhn was. Whereas Kuhn was a technically busy pianist who frequently matched phrases with Coltrane during the tenor player's solos, Tyner, who had a more rhythmic approach to the instrument, spent more time comping—playing chords to provide a platform on which others could build solos. Sometimes Tyner would lay out completely during others' solos, something Kuhn would rarely if ever do, and Coltrane liked this. Also, Kuhn had a refined, almost delicate style, while Tyner was more dynamic. At times, Tyner used large chords, producing an almost orchestral richness. He could also be very percussive in his approach, patterning his work closely with that of the drummer. Although both Kuhn and Tyner had flawless technique, Kuhn preferred to dazzle the listener, saying as much as possible in a short space, whereas Tyner was expansive and inclined to powerful understatement.

Significantly, the replacement of Kuhn with Tyner is entirely consistent with Coltrane's interest in the drumming of Elvin Jones, who like Tyner had a powerful yet always subtle approach to his instrument. Coltrane's deep respect and appreciation for these two musicians and his desire to play with them is evidence that, virtually from the onset of his career as a bandleader, Coltrane was seeking a specific sound. And when Jones joined the group later, that sound was brilliantly realized.

The current group played a short stint at Small's Paradise in Harlem and then returned to the Gallery for two more weeks. One night, Coltrane and Eric Dolphy, an outstanding sax player and one of his closest friends, sat in with Ornette Coleman's band at the Five Spot. Dolphy, who had mastered the flute, bass clarinet, and alto saxophone, had played for some time with bassist/composer Charles Mingus. After the gig, John, Eric, and Ornette went to Coleman's apartment in the East Village to talk music. For Coltrane, this reunion sparked a renewed interest in Coleman's har-melodic theory.

The group hit the road in Coltrane's Mercury station wagon, heading west and playing gigs along the way. Before leaving New York, John had told Naima that he had become unhappy with LaRoca's playing. When the band reached Detroit, he gave the drummer severance pay and plane fare back to New York. He then replaced LaRoca with Billy Higgins, who had played most recently with Ornette Coleman.

But Coltrane was still not satisfied. While LaRoca's style was to play just behind the beat, Higgins played directly on the beat. For Coltrane, neither was right. What he wanted was a drummer who played slightly ahead of the beat, to propel the music forward. What he wanted was Elvin Jones.

One night in Los Angeles, Coltrane ran into Thad Jones, Elvin's brother, who told him that Elvin was out of jail, so John should give him a call. After numerous unsuccessful attempts, Coltrane finally reached the drummer and extended an invitation. Elvin eagerly accepted, and Higgins was out. Elvin agreed to join up with the band in Denver, Colorado. When he arrived, he found a brand-new drum set waiting for him, compliments of John Coltrane.

Elvin Jones studied the drums privately while he was in high school. After thinking about becoming a doctor, he decided on a career in music and left school after the tenth grade. He worked at odd jobs while continuing his drum lessons with private teachers. His hard-driving, complex playing made an incredible difference in the sound of the John Coltrane Quartet. Jones had the astonishing ability to keep several rhythms going at the same time, with a force that a listener felt deep in his chest. With the raw energy of Jones behind the drums, Coltrane finally had the band he wanted.

At the Half Note in New York, Coltrane howled and wailed above a deluge of rhythm and harmony. By now he had absorbed the various kinds of ethnic music he had explored in recent years, and his particular blending of these influences became his signature. Spewing out drones, trills, squeals, and honks in sheets, Coltrane thrived in the setting of the new quartet. Even the critics recognized his newfound inspiration: Among all jazz tenor players, Coltrane placed second, behind Coleman Hawkins, in the International Critics Poll in the August 8, 1960, issue of *Down Beat*. In the October 10 issue, Coltrane placed first in the saxophone category of the *Down Beat* readers' poll. For obvious reasons, he was eager to bring the group into the recording studio. In October 1960, the band recorded *My Favorite Things* for the Atlantic label. The record sold more than fifty thousand copies in the first year of its release, an extraordinary commercial success for a jazz album at the time. One jazz critic reviewed the album in the San Francisco *Examiner*:

> *It is, without question, the best Coltrane album to date, and almost*
> *equally without question, one of the most important of the 1960s. . . .*
> *If one listens to Trane's long, complex solo, then follows through and*
> *hears how skillfully pianist McCoy Tyner lays an implacable founda-*

tion for Coltrane's second—complex, masterful, and exceedingly logi-
cal—solo, it becomes apparent that marvelous things have happened to
the Coltrane horn.

Another critic wrote in the Minneapolis *Sunday Tribune*:

Coltrane is not an artist you can listen to casually. You must give him
your undivided attention to even begin to appreciate his talent. He
emits a stream of musical consciousness that could, I suppose, be
likened to some of the writings of James Joyce.

He produces music that might be incomprehensible to some listen-
ers, but its value and meaning lie in his compulsion to weave an en-
tire piece of musical cloth almost instantaneously. . . . My Favorite
Things *is one of his best recordings.*

Improving on such a band would seem impossible, but Coltrane made
another change in the group's personnel as 1960 ended: He replaced Steve
Davis with the bassist Reggie Workman.

That year, the civil rights movement that was born in the 1950s began
to gain momentum throughout the United States. As the 1960s began,
African-Americans still struggled to survive in a society that allowed them
access to only substandard education, deteriorating housing, and low-pay-
ing jobs. Few blacks received adequate medical care, and the infant sur-
vival rate for blacks was well below average. At the heart of the problem
was racism and the policies of racial segregation, so African-Americans
took to the streets in increasing numbers throughout the 1960s and engaged
in civil disobedience to protest the injustices of racial discrimination.

One well-known incident of civil disobedience occurred in February
1960, when four black college freshmen in Greensboro, North Carolina,
sat down at a restaurant counter and ordered something to eat. They were
denied service by the owner because they were black. Although they
were insulted and taunted by the white patrons at the store, the students
remained at the counter and demanded to be served. Rather than give in

to the students' demands, the owner closed the counter for the day. The next day the students returned, and again each day after that until they were finally served at the counter.

Another well-known incident took place in May 1961, when black and white "freedom riders" traveled by bus throughout the South, using "whites only" rest rooms and lunch counters along the way. They intended to demonstrate peacefully at every stop along their journey from Washington, D.C., to New Orleans, Louisiana, but they clashed with racists at almost every turn. In Anniston, Alabama, one of their buses was smashed and set on fire with the freedom riders still inside. The attackers held the doors of the bus closed as the people inside struggled to escape from the burning vehicle. When they finally did escape, just before the bus exploded, the demonstrators were beaten with baseball bats, pipes, and chains. Similar incidents took place in Birmingham and Montgomery, Alabama, as well as in other states along the way. Local police officials rarely made any attempt to stop the violence.

A number of jazz critics tried to place the new music coming out of the jazz scene, particularly as played by African-American musicians, in the context of the civil unrest that was spreading across the country. This was the impetus for describing Coltrane and other black tenor saxophonists of the day as "the angry young tenors." But Coltrane denied that his music had any real political content and took exception to the label "angry young tenors." He explained that he was trying to grow, both as a musician and as a person, and along the way to create as much beautiful music as he could. Still, Coltrane realized the power of music to bring about change. He had this to say to the writer Frank Kofsky in 1966:

> *[Jazz] is an expression of higher ideals, to me. So brotherhood is there; and I believe with brotherhood, there would be no poverty. And also with brotherhood, there would be no war.*

In the same interview Coltrane went on to say,

I want to be a force for real good. In other words, I know that there are bad forces, forces out here that bring suffering to others and misery to the world, but I want to be the force which is truly for good.

Unlike Miles Davis, Coltrane gave very few specific instructions to the musicians in his band. It was up to each individual player to sense instinctively what Coltrane wanted to hear. Those who failed to do this—Steve Kuhn and Billy Higgins, for example—were asked to leave the group. Before long, Reggie Workman, too, began to struggle under the demands of the quartet, and Coltrane added a second bassist, Arthur Davis.

In 1961, Coltrane left Atlantic and signed with the fledgling Impulse! label. His contract with Impulse! made Coltrane the second-highest-paid recording artist in jazz (second to Miles Davis). It called for a minimum of two albums a year for three years, and he would be paid $50,000 in installments.

For his first album on Impulse!, Coltrane expanded the group further, adding a number of horns, including a tuba, and he invited his close friend Eric Dolphy to sit in on the sessions. The result was *Africa Brass*, an exotic album of distinctively African musical forays. Elvin Jones thrived in this setting, and a powerful rendition of the tune "Greensleeves" came out of the sessions. Also that year, the Atlantic label released the Coltrane album *My Favorite Things,* which featured a rendition the waltz of that name from Rodgers and Hammerstein's show *The Sound of Music.* The album eventually went gold, a rare accomplishment for a jazz album during the 1960s.

On November 2, 3, and 5, the group played the Village Vanguard, a renowned New York jazz venue, and recorded the sets live. Jimmy Garrison sat in for Art Davis, who was not available to play those dates. Included on *"Live" at the Village Vanguard* were the Coltrane originals "India," "Impressions," and "Spiritual," as well as a remarkable group blues improvisation entitled "Chasin' the Trane," which is based on a theme by the French composer Claude Debussy and runs for the entire second side of the album. With these pieces, which incorporated Indian ragas and other

Coltrane on soprano sax

non-Western musical forms, the quartet had clearly moved well beyond the conventions of modern jazz toward something more Eastern, more spiritual. After the Vanguard shows, the band toured Europe.

When the group returned from Europe in December, Reggie Workman was drafted into the military. He refused to report, stating that he would not fight for a country whose policies he did not believe in, but the trouble that followed, combined with his father's illness, forced him to take leave from the band. Coltrane promptly replaced Workman with his old friend Jimmy Garrison, who had become a phenomenal bass stylist in recent years playing with Ornette Coleman. Like Coltrane, Garrison was also an extremely hard worker, often practicing until his hands were too swollen to continue. The new group recorded three albums for Impulse! during 1962: *Coltrane, Ballads*, and *Duke Ellington and John Coltrane*.

Duke Ellington and John Coltrane, recorded in September 1962, is surprising in that Coltrane's playing is strangely refined and elegant. The sound is still Coltrane, but the restraint clearly evidences the deep respect he had for the Duke and his music. Coltrane's solos on this date, though staying uncharacteristically close to the melody, nonetheless carry his signature. The tenorman treads lightly over Ellington's piano accompaniment, carefully preserving the purity of the composer's musical ideas. Saxophone great Johnny Hodges, who for decades was the featured soloist on "In a Sentimental Mood" while he played in the Ellington band, said, "As long as I've known this song, I think Coltrane gave the most beautiful interpretation I've ever heard."

By 1963, John and Naima had developed problems in their relationship, and he had strayed from the marriage. While touring Europe with the quartet in the fall, Coltrane met a woman named Randi Hultin, and the two quickly developed an intimate relationship.

Meanwhile, America was in a state of social and political upheaval as civil rights demonstrations increasingly turned violent. In September 1962, for example, racist protesters clashed with federal marshals in Mississippi when a black Air Force veteran named James Meredith tried to become the first black student to enroll at the University of Mississippi. Another incident occurred in the spring of 1963, when a peaceful demonstration in Birmingham, Alabama, led by Dr. Martin Luther King, Jr., turned violent. King was thrown in jail, where he wrote his "Letter from a Birmingham Jail," perhaps the most eloquent expression of the philosophy and goals of the civil rights movement. Then in May 1963, some three thousand young people marched into downtown Birmingham, carrying banners and singing songs for freedom. On the orders of the sheriff, high-pressure fire hoses were turned on the demonstrators, prompting them to hold a mass prayer meeting in front of the Birmingham jail. On the television news, Americans were outraged as they watched vicious police dogs biting black women, and schoolchildren being thrown into buildings and cars by the force of the blasts from fire hoses. Still, Governor George Wallace of Alabama shouted his motto, "Segregation Now! Segregation Tomorrow! Segregation Forever!" and vowed to block the registration of black students at Alabama State University. Eventually, with the help of federal marshals, the students registered. The violence in Alabama continued, however, and in September 1963 four black girls were killed when a Baptist church in Birmingham was bombed by the Ku Klux Klan, a militant white racist group. At the funeral, Dr. King delivered the eulogy, in which he called the four girls "heroines of a holy crusade for freedom and human dignity."

On August 28, 1963, the movement to end violence and racism had perhaps its most shining moment, when more than 200,000 pro-civil rights activists, black and white, marched on Washington, D.C.; Dr. King delivered his "I Had a Dream" speech, calling for an end to racial segregation and the coming together of all people in the name of brotherhood. The following year, Congress passed a civil rights bill, making segregation illegal.

One prominent civil rights activist was Malcolm X Shabazz. In 1964, Malcolm X, as he was known, was making speeches in an effort to organize black people into a political force. Coltrane attended one of the speeches and was impressed with both the man's ideas and his passion for social change. But the political arena was not Coltrane's venue. His path was essentially an inner one. When the group emerged from the recording studio in December with the masterpiece *A Love Supreme,* there was no doubt of that. Still, there was undeniable truth in the pianist Cecil Taylor's remark, "Coltrane has a feeling for the hysteria of the times."

CHAPTER EIGHT

OM . . .

In 1963, Coltrane was reunited with another musician who would play a central role in his life. Her name was Alice McLeod. A tall, shy woman from Detroit, Michigan, McLeod studied piano with the great Bud Powell. She first met Coltrane at a party in 1960, and on July 18, 1963, they met again at Birdland, where both their bands were on the bill.

John and Alice moved into a house in the Dix Hills section of Huntington, Long Island. From his dates and his recordings, Coltrane was making very good money now and was able to furnish the new ten-room house promptly. His first purchase was a grand piano, and he also bought a harp, which Alice had recently begun to study.

On a typical morning, Coltrane rose before dawn, wrapped himself in a silk bathrobe, and went to his study. There he sat cross-legged on the floor and breathed deeply, relaxing his mind and body. He often emerged from several hours of meditation with new musical ideas. One such musical idea was the essential theme of *A Love Supreme*, which Coltrane said was his humble offering to God.

Coltrane's mother was worried about her son. Before writing the music for *A Love Supreme*, John had told her about a profound mystical experience he had—a vision of God. He also said that he had recently seen other such

John and Alice Coltrane work at the piano in Newport, Rhode Island, in 1966.

visions while playing. She was worried because, as she said, "When someone is seeing God, that means he's going to die."

After *A Love Supreme*, Coltrane's music became even more free and deeply personal. The albums *Ascension* (with Pharoah Sanders and Archie Shepp joining Coltrane on tenor saxophones), *Transition, Sun Ship, Infinity, OM,* and *Meditations* show Coltrane's turn to mysticism. Spirituality was now at the center of his music, and he was consumed by one goal—to know

A Love Supreme *(album cover)*

God. Soon after Coltrane recorded *Meditations,* a critic asked him to talk about the music. He responded:

> *Once you become aware of this force for unity in life, you can't ever forget it. It becomes part of everything you do. In that respect, this* [Meditations] *is an extension of* A Love Supreme *since my conception of that force keeps changing shape. My goal in meditating on this through music, however, remains the same. And that is to uplift people, as much as I can. To inspire them to realize more and more of their capacities for living meaningful lives. Because there is certainly meaning to life.*

Meanwhile, the United States was fighting a war in Vietnam. When asked in an interview for his thoughts on the war, Coltrane said, "I am opposed to war; therefore I am opposed to the Vietnam War. I think all wars should be stopped." At one point, tears filled his eyes, and he asked the interviewer, "Why can't people learn to love each other?"

On July 26 and 27, 1965, the quartet played the Antibes Jazz Festival in Juan-Les-Pins, France, and then moved on to Paris. But back home, the violence continued. The black nationalist Malcolm X had been brutally murdered on February 21, and by the summer the anger in the African-American community had reached a feverish pitch nationwide. On August 11, 1965, in the Watts section of Los Angeles, California, 33 people were killed, 812 injured, and more than 3,000 arrested in six days of rioting. When Coltrane heard about the rioting in Watts, he phoned Eric Dolphy's parents, who lived there (Dolphy had died the year before), just to make sure they were all right.

That year, Coltrane was showered with accolades by the editors and critics at *Down Beat* magazine, who named him jazzman of the year and elected him to its Hall of Fame. *A Love Supreme* was selected by the magazine's editors as record of the year, a distinction also bestowed on the album by the International Critics Poll. The critics also named Coltrane the number-two soprano sax player in the world (behind Steve Lacy).

John was on the move in his personal life as well in 1965. After he and Naima were divorced, John and Alice were married in Juarez, Mexico. Eventually, the couple would have three children together, all boys—John, Jr., Ravi, and Oran. They named Ravi after the Indian sitar virtuoso Ravi Shankar, although they had never met him. When Coltrane and Shankar met each other in November 1965, the jazzman listened closely while the master of the raga spoke about India's rich musical heritage. (Although they are quite different, jazz and Indian music share the element of improvisation.) Coltrane held a deep appreciation for Shankar's music, but the sitarist had this to say about Coltrane's playing:

> *I was much disturbed by his music. Here was a creative person who had become a vegetarian, who was studying yoga and reading the* Bhagavad-Gita, *yet in whose music I still heard much turmoil. I could not understand it. . . . The music was fantastic. I was much impressed, but one thing distressed me. There was a turbulence in the music that gave me a negative feeling at times, but I could not quite put my finger on the trouble.*

Still, the two musicians crossed both musical and cultural barriers and became very good friends.

Meanwhile, Coltrane's band continued to evolve. In December, McCoy Tyner left the group to lead his own band and follow his own musical direction, and Alice took his place. A second drummer, Rashied Ali, was added too. Then, unhappy about having to share the groove with another drummer, Jones left the band and joined Duke Ellington. In July 1966, Coltrane and his new band were recorded live at the Village Vanguard and then toured Japan.

Coltrane was idolized in Japan, and when his plane landed at Tokyo International Airport on July 8, thousands of Japanese greeted him. Each of his albums had sold some 300,000 copies in Japan, but the Japanese not only loved Coltrane's music, they also adored Coltrane personally. His

Coltrane practices the flute while on a flight to Tokyo, Japan, in 1966.

humble dress and manner despite his remarkable talent gave him an almost saint-like aura among the Japanese, who have traditionally had a high regard for soft-spoken humility. Fans stopped John and Alice in the streets of Japan's major cities, sometimes asking him to sign their shirts. Alice Coltrane later told the story about how a Japanese boy followed her and her husband's taxi on foot for several miles just to get John's autograph. Every show in Japan was a whopping success, and Coltrane spread his message of love, peace, and brotherhood at every stop, not only with his music but also by his gentle example.

Upon his return to New York in early 1967, Coltrane and the band once again played the Village Vanguard. Also that year, Coltrane formed his own record company, Jowcol, and recorded several musical explorations on this label, including one named after and dedicated to Martin Luther King, Jr. In April, Coltrane played two shows at the Olatunji Center of African Culture in New York on the theme of Roots of Africa. Coltrane insisted that the price of admission to the shows be low enough so that just about anyone could afford to attend.

Around this time, Coltrane began to complain of stomach problems and headaches. When Alice suggested he see a doctor, John refused and returned to his obsessive work schedule. He also renewed his contract with the Impulse! label, signing a two-year deal, and made plans to go into the studio. Then, in May, while he and Alice were visiting his mother, John doubled over in pain, clutching his stomach and groaning. He made his way to a bedroom and emerged, apparently recovered, an hour later. When the couple returned to their house on Long Island, Alice made a doctor's appointment for her husband. He was examined and checked into a hospital, where a biopsy was taken, but he refused to stay on for more testing, despite his doctor's recommendation.

On Sunday morning, July 16, 1967, Coltrane was rushed to the emergency room of Huntington Hospital. He looked up from his hospital bed, clutching his wife's hand. He died there at 4:00 the next morning, of liver cancer. Coltrane's admirers crowded into St. Peter's Lutheran Church in New York for the memorial services, at the end of which Ornette Coleman played the tune "Holiday for a Graveyard" in honor of his good friend John Coltrane.

As Coltrane's body was lowered into his grave at Pinelawn Memorial Park in Farmingdale, New York, violence continued to rock America's cities and college campuses. People increasingly took to the streets to speak out against oppression and the madness of war. The country's value system was in an upheaval as America's young people rebelled. They grew their hair long; wore shredded jeans, tie-dyed shirts, sandals, and beads;

Jazz resounded through the church at John Coltrane's funeral on July 17, 1967.

experimented with drugs and new sexual freedoms; advocated a return to ecological awareness and peace; tried alternative, communal living arrangements and family structures; and adopted left-wing political ideas. Their parents' generation, they believed, had veered dangerously off course, and the country needed to be put back on the right track. There was much disagreement about which track was the right one, however.

During the late 1960s, the arts reflected the turmoil in the United States. The literary fare of the day included the so-called beat poetry of Allen Ginsberg and Gary Snyder; the anti-novels of Jack Kerouac and William

John Coltrane's body rests at the Pinelawn Memorial Park, Long Island, New York.

Burroughs; and the philosophy of the East. In the world of dance, Twyla Tharp and Merce Cunningham were experimenting with random and unorthodox movements. Contemporary visual artists such as Andy Warhol turned their backs on the established abstract expressionist forms to create junk art and pop art, incorporating everyday images and objects from popular and commercial culture. The serious popular music spectrum ranged from the existential folk protests of Bob Dylan to the psychedelic electric rock of Jefferson Airplane and the Grateful Dead. The Beatles, who had revolutionized pop music by launching the so-called British invasion of the early 1960s, opened new doors with the 1967 release of their album *Sergeant Pepper's Lonely Hearts Club Band*. In the world of jazz, a handful of artists had broken down the barriers established by bebop, and Coltrane was foremost among them.

More than simply dramatically changing the music, John Coltrane transformed the very idea of what it was to be a jazz musician. Although

Coltrane strayed into the seedy underworld of jazz for a time, ultimately he smashed the stereotype of the fast-living, drug-shooting, alcoholic jazz genius, which Charlie Parker epitomized. Coltrane was both jazz virtuoso and spiritual seeker, combining a wealth of musical knowledge and a razor-sharp technique with a strict, even monastic work ethic and a deep faith in the existence of a higher power. His sound was a lonely wail in the night, hoping, searching, reaching into the darkness. For Coltrane, life was the interplay of music, love, and the divine, which at certain creative moments one realizes are three words for the same thing.

TIMELINE
IMPORTANT EVENTS
IN THE LIFE OF
JOHN COLTRANE

1926 Born John William Coltrane in Hamlet, North Carolina, on September 23

1932 Enrolls at Leonard Street Elementary School

1939 Father dies on January 2; enrolls at the William Penn High School; plays alto horn and later clarinet in community band

1940 Begins playing alto saxophone

1942 Joins the newly formed William Penn High School band

1943 Graduates from William Penn and moves to Philadelphia

1944 Enrolls at the Ornstein School of Music

1945 Begins to play professionally; joins the Navy and is stationed on Oahu, Hawaii

1946 Discharged from the Navy; returns to Philadelphia

1947 Begins studies with Dennis Sandole and Matthew Rastelli at the Granoff Studio
Begins association with Eddie "Cleanhead" Vinson

1949 Begins association with trumpeter Dizzy Gillespie

1953 Begins association with saxophonist Johnny Hodges; meets Naima Austin (first wife)

1955 Begins association with trumpeter Miles Davis; marries Naima on October 3

1957 Begins association with pianist Thelonious Monk

1958 Sheila Coltrane (daughter) born

1959 Records *Kind of Blue*, with the Miles Davis Sextet, and *Giant Steps*, his first record as a leader

1960 Records *My Favorite Things*

1961 Collaborates with saxophonist Eric Dolphy

1962 Establishes the "classic quartet" with McCoy Tyner, Jimmy Garrison, and Elvin Jones

1963 Meets Alice McLeod (second wife)

1964 Records *A Love Supreme*; John Coltrane, Jr., born on August 26 to Alice McLoed

1965 Ravi Coltrane (son) born on August 6 to Alice McLoed

1966 Divorces Naima; marries Alice McLeod

1967 Oran (son) born on March 19 to John and Alice Coltrane; John Coltrane dies of liver cancer on July 17

FOR FURTHER INFORMATION

Books

Carr, Roy. *A Century of Jazz: From Blues to Bop, Swing to Hiphop—A Hundred Years of Music, Musicians, Swingers, and Styles.* New York: De Capo Press, 1997.

Collier, James Lincoln. *Jazz: An American Saga.* New York: Henry Holt, 1997.

Cooke, Mervyn. *The Chronicle of Jazz.* New York: Abbeville Press, 1998.

Crisp, George R. *Miles Davis.* Danbury, CT: Franklin Watts, 1997.

Fitterling, Thomas. *Thelonius Monk: His Life and Music.* Berkeley, CA: Berkeley Hills Books, 1997.

Fraim, John. *Spirit Catcher: The Life and Art of John Coltrane.* West Liberty, OH: Greathouse, 1996.

Gourse, Leslie. *Blowing on the Changes: The Art of the Jazz Horn Players.* Danbury, CT: Franklin Watts, 1997.

Nisenson, Eric. *Ascension: John Coltrane and His Quest.* New York: St. Martin's Press, 1993.

Porter, Lewis. *John Coltrane: His Life and Music.* Ann Arbor, MI: University of Michigan Press, 1998.

Vail, Ken. *Jazz Milestones: A Pictorial Chronicle of Jazz 1900–1990.* Detroit: Omnigraphics, 1996.

Videos

The World According to John Coltrane, BMG Video (59 min.)

The Coltrane Legacy, VAI Video (61 min.)

Organizations and Online Sites

All About Jazz: A Magazine for Jazz Fans by Jazz Fans

http://www.allaboutjazz.com

Some of the highlights of this site are two weekly features, "Spotlight Site of the Week" and "Jazz Journalist of the Week," and "Fun Stuff," a link that includes jazz trivia, a Who's Who Gallery, musical terms, and a name pronunciation guide.

Blue Note Records

http://www.bluenote.com/artistpage.asp?ArtistID=3405

A page devoted to Coltrane on the Blue Note website, including a short biography and links to track listings for all of Coltrane's Blue Note discs. Also links to the Blue Note main website, with volumes of information about jazz, past and present, and the Blue Note catalog.

International Saxophone Page

http://www.saxophone.org

Includes comprehensive information on the instrument as well as current reviews, articles, news, interviews, and links.

Internet Jazz Hall of Fame

http://www.jazzhall.org

Features include a "Jazz Time Line" that defines each major jazz style, a searchable database for favorite muscians, songwriters, bandleaders, and singers, and a message board.

John Coltrane: A Love Supreme

http://jazz.route66.net/aLoveSupreme/

Extensive tribute site to Coltrane, including biography, photos, discography, and more.

John Coltrane Listserv

http://www.netaxs.com/~jgreshes/lists/coltrane-l.html

This website provides instructions on how to join an ongoing listserv discussion on the life and works of John Coltrane.

The John W. Coltrane Cultural Center
1511 N. 33rd Street
Philadelphia, PA 19121

A Philadelphia cultural center that runs community programs to help improve the lives and cultural awareness of young people in Philadelphia.

What John Coltrane Wanted

http://www.theatlantic.com/unbound/jazz/strickla.htm

Article by Edward Strickland maintained in the *Atlantic Monthly* website archives that explores Coltrane's spiritual commitment to his music.

SELECTED
DISCOGRAPHY

Note: Many of John Coltrane's recordings have been remastered and reissued by companies other than the original recording label. In this discography, the original recording label and year is noted first, followed by a parenthetical reference to the reissuing label and year.

Recordings by John Coltrane

Afro Blue Impressions. Originally recorded by Pablo, 1963 (Fantasy, 1993).

Art of John Coltrane. Originally recorded by Blue Note, 1956-57 (EMD/Blue Note, 1992).

The Avant-Garde. Originally recorded by Atlantic, 1960 (Fantasy, 1990).

Bahia. Originally recorded by Prestige, 1958 (Fantasy, 1990).

The Believer. Originally recorded by Prestige, 1958 (Fantasy, 1996).

The Best of John Coltrane. Originally recorded by Atlantic, 1959-60 (WEA/Atlantic, 1990).

The Best of John Coltrane. Originally recorded by Pablo, 1963 (Fantasy 1991).

Black Pearls. Originally recorded by Prestige, 1958 (Fantasy, 1989).

Blue Train. Originally recorded by Blue Note, 1957 (EMD/Blue Note, 1990).

Blue Trane: John Coltrane Plays the Blues. Originally recorded by Prestige, 1957-58 (Fantasy, 1996).

Bye Bye Blackbird. Originally recorded by Pablo, 1962 (Fantasy, 1992).

Coltrane 7105. Originally recorded by Prestige, 1957 (Fantasy 1987).

Coltrane Jazz. Originally recorded by Atlantic, 1959 (WEA/Atlantic, 1990).

Coltrane Plays the Blues. Originally recorded by Atlantic, 1960 (WEA/Atlantic, 1990).

Coltrane's Sound. Originally recorded by Atlantic, 1960 (WEA/Atlantic, 1999).

Coltrane Time. Originally recorded by United Artists in 1959 as a Cecil Taylor album (entitled *Stereo Drive*). Originally recorded by Blue Note, 1962 (EMD/Blue Note, 1991).

Dakar. Originally recorded by Prestige, 1957 (Fantasy, 1989).

First Meditations. Originally recorded by Impulse!, 1965 (UNI/Impulse, 1992).

Gentle Side of John Coltrane. Originally recorded by Impulse!, 1961–64 (UNI/Impulse, 1991).

Giant Steps. Originally recorded by Atlantic, 1959 (WEA/Atlantic, 1998).

Like Sonny. Originally recorded by Blue Note, 1960 (EMD/Blue Note, 1990).

"Live" at the Village Vanguard. Originally recorded by Impulse!, 1961 (UNI/Impulse, 1998).

A Love Supreme. Originally recorded by Impulse!, 1964 (UNI/Impulse, 1995).

Lush Life. Originally recorded by Prestige, 1958 (Fantasy, 1987).

Meditations. Originally recorded by Impulse!, 1966 (UNI/Impulse, 1996).

My Favorite Things. Originally recorded by Atlantic, 1960 (WEA/Atlantic, 1998).

Olé Coltrane. Originally recorded by Atlantic, 1961 (WEA/Atlantic, 1990).

The Paris Concert. Originally recorded by Pablo, 1961-62 (Fantasy, 1993).

Soultrane. Originally recorded by Prestige, 1958 (Fantasy, 1987).

Anthologies

The Complete 1961 Village Vanguard Recordings (UNI/Impulse, 1997).

The Heavyweight Champion: The Complete Atlantic Recordings of John Coltrane. Originally recorded by Atlantic, 1959–61 (WEA/Atlantic, 1995).

A John Coltrane Restrospective: The Impulse! Years. Originally recorded by Impulse!, 1961–65 (UNI/Impulse, 1992).

The Last Giant: The John Coltrane Anthology. Originally recorded by Atlantic, 1946–67 (WEA/Atlantic, 1993).

Recordings by the John Coltrane Quartet

Ballads. Originally recorded by Impulse!, 1962 (UNI/Impulse, 1995).

Classic Quartet—Complete Impulse! Studio Recordings. Originally recorded by Impulse!, 1961–65 (Fantasy, 1998).

Coltrane. Originally recorded by Impulse!, 1962 (UNI/Impulse, 1997).

The Complete Africa/Brass Sessions. Originally recorded by Impulse!, 1961 (UNI/Impulse, 1995).

Crescent. Originally recorded by Impulse!, 1964 (UNI/Impulse, 1996).

The John Coltrane Quartet Plays. Originally recorded by Impulse!, 1965 (UNI/Impulse, 1997).

Live at Birdland. Originally recorded by Impulse!, 1964 (UNI/Impulse, 1996).

A New Thing at Newport. The John Coltrane Quartet with Archie Shepp. Originally recorded by Impulse!, 1965 (UNI/Impulse, 1991).

Other Recordings

Cannonball & Coltrane. With Cannonball Adderly. Originally recorded by Emarcy, 1959 (PGD/Verve 1988).

Circle in the Round. With Miles Davis. Originally recorded by CBS Records, 1955–70 (Sony, 1991).

Cookin' with the Miles Davis Quintet. With Miles Davis. Originally recorded by Prestige, 1956 (Fantasy, 1985).

Duke Ellington & John Coltrane. With Duke Ellington. Originally recorded by Impulse!, 1962 (UNI/Impulse, 1995).

High Pressure: The Red Garland Quintet with John Coltrane. Originally recorded by Prestige, 1958 (Fantasy, 1989).

John Coltrane and Johnny Hartman. With Johnny Hartman. Originally recorded by Impulse!, 1962–63 (UNI/Impulse, 1995).

Kind of Blue. With Miles Davis. Originally recorded by Columbia, 1959 (Sony, 1997).

Live at the Five Spot Discovery! With Thelonius Monk. Originally recorded by Blue Note, 1958 (EMD/Blue Note, 1993).

Miles. With Miles Davis. Originally recorded by Prestige, 1955 (DCC Gold Disc, 1996).

Milestones. With Miles Davis. Originally recorded by Columbia, 1958 (Sony, 1990).

Monk's Music. With Thelonius Monk. Originally recorded by Riverside, 1957 (Fantasy, 1987).

Relaxin' with the Miles Davis Quintet. With Miles Davis. Originally recorded by Prestige, 1956 (Fantasy, 1991).

Someday My Prince Will Come. With Miles Davis. Originally recorded by Columbia, 1961 (Sony, 1990).

Steamin' with the Miles Davis Quintet. With Miles Davis. Originally recorded by Prestige, 1956 (Fantasy, 1989).

Thelonius Himself. With Thelonius Monk. Originally recorded by Riverside, 1957 (Fantasy, 1987).

Thelonius Monk with John Coltrane. Originally recorded by Prestige, 1957 (Fantasy, 1987).

Traneing In: John Coltrane with the Red Garland Trio. Originally recorded by Prestige, 1957 (Fantasy, 1987).

Workin' with the Miles Davis Quintet. With Miles Davis. Originally recorded by Prestige, 1956 (Fantasy, 1990).

INDEX

ABOUT THE AUTHOR

John Selfridge is a writer, editor, and book publisher with an insatiable appetite for great jazz. A graduate of Drew University, Columbia University Teachers College, and Rutgers Law School, Mr. Selfridge is also an amateur musician, or, as he calls himself, a hopelessly unaccomplished multi-instrumentalist. This is his sixth book and his first on a jazz subject.